THE
SARTORIAL
TRAVEL GUIDE

SIMON CROMPTON

WITH 213 ILLUSTRATIONS

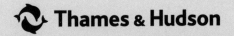

Contents

Introduction

When I was younger, one of my favourite aspects of travel was finding small local shops in different European cities and bringing back functional souvenirs. Olive-wood boards from Mallorca. Timepieces from Switzerland. Kitchen knives from France. They made my house characterful and personal, and collecting them was one of the real pleasures of going abroad.

I remember discovering a beautiful shop in a small town outside Barcelona that sold crafts made by artisans from around Catalonia. The proprietor had purposefully collected together only the finest makers and brands, and the curation was wonderful. I walked away with an armful.

Over the years, this sort of shop became harder to find, both at home and abroad. Easier access to products through e-commerce and mail-order was the biggest culprit, but many local makers were also consciously expanding, selling into more stores, whether bricks-and-mortar or online. Suddenly every brand was everywhere.

It was a few years before I started writing about menswear, but I quickly realized that there the problem was even worse. The fast and easy visual communication of fashion and the large marketing budgets of designer brands were pushing everyone into rapid expansion. The trend was most obvious in China, where new brands were opening a dozen stores at a time. Even for smaller start-ups, the plan was to launch a brand, quickly add multiple shops around a city, and then expand around the world.

Now there was very little that you had to travel to see. That core attraction of travel – encountering not just unique local culture, architecture and natural wonders, but also local retail – had largely disappeared.

In recent years, the tide has slowly started to turn. New shops are

OPPOSITE There is no substitute for visiting a shop in person, holdling the products with your own hands, and learning about them from experienced staff and makers.

prioritizing the things that online retail can't offer: face-to-face interaction with customers, unique and beautiful physical shop environments and the tactile pleasure of handling the products. Unlike large international chains, the sartorial focus of these new independent shops and local chains is on their own region, city or even neighbourhood. Stores like The Armoury in Hong Kong or Trunk Clothiers in London, both of which opened in the past decade, have developed passionate local followings and their own unique aesthetic.

Old shops, too, are being rediscovered. Italy and Germany, with their large regional cities, always had the best selection of independent shops and makers, some of which thankfully survive. Their emphasis on traditional craftsmanship and distinctive customer experience is slowly attracting a new generation. This is particularly the case with bespoke craftsmen such as tailors or shoemakers. Many of them travel the world doing trunk shows, but dedicated customers always want to visit the original atelier, to drink in the heritage and see where their garments are made. There is real depth to those local roots.

For the past ten years, I've written about many of these shops on my website PermanentStyle.com. But I haven't seen a good guide to them: a publication that lists the best stores, explains what is unique about each one, and gives the reader a reason to travel.

The Sartorial Travel Guide was born out of a desire to produce a targeted, pocket-sized guide to the best menswear stores around the world – and in the process, to encourage the trend towards high-quality, customer-oriented retail.

The main body of the guide explores ten of the world's best cities for menswear, mapping and listing contact details for the most interesting

OPPOSITE ABOVE
The author being fitted
for a kimono at Motoji
in Tokyo.

OPPOSITE BELOW
The author visiting
bespoke tailor
Vestrucci in Florence.

shops in each city, followed by detailed profiles of a few of them. A further 15 'must-see' shops in other cities are highly recommended if you have the opportunity for a visit as part of a quick day-trip or a long flight layover.

These are all stores I know personally and have visited frequently. Their descriptions in this book therefore often centre on my own experience, which makes them a bit subjective, but also allows space to talk about the process of being measured for a kimono, or of finding the hidden artisans of Naples.

Historic ateliers and flagships of a few globally recognized names – such as Hermès in Paris and Armani in Milan – have been included because they are uniquely rooted in the sartorial culture of their native cities and offer a shopping experience that can't be found in branches elsewhere in the world. Otherwise, the focus of the selection is on independent shops selling quality menswear,

with a leaning towards classic style, tailored and bespoke. There are a few recommendations for workwear and country clothing, but this is essentially a sartorial guide.

I've also included contributions from some of the world's most knowledgeable people on menswear and travel – buyers, editors, stylists and journalists – who share travel tips, techniques for scouting out new stores, and their insights on the fashion industry. I conclude with two practical pieces offering advice on assembling a capsule wardrobe for travelling, and fitting it all neatly into a suitcase.

This is a not simply a guide to finding the world's best menswear, but to rediscovering the joy of independent shopping wherever you travel. I hope I have given you everything you need to enjoy the journey.

Simon Crompton

Sartorial Travel Tips from the Experts

How to Enjoy Travel

Mark Cho

The Armoury, Hong Kong and New York

Between the three branches of The Armoury in New York and Hong Kong, and Drake's headquarters in London, Mark is always globetrotting. He shares his tips for making travelling easier, more efficient and more enjoyable.

I log an average of 40 flight hours every month, and life on the road is something I've come to embrace. While most people love the idea of travelling, the actual time spent in transit or on long-haul flights is often something they dread. I don't think it has to be that way.

I only travel with clamshell-style Rimowa suitcases. I pack all my trousers first, stacking them in one side of the case so that the waistband goes on alternate sides. I then place my folded jackets on top, alternating on which side the collar goes. This leaves a little void in the corners, enough to tuck in two pairs of shoes and some socks and underwear. I put everything else in the other side of the case.

I don't like getting wrinkles in my ties. Ties should never be pressed but steam does not always make wrinkles fall out easily. To avoid my ties wrinkling in the first place, I use old Drake's tie boxes to transport them. They are rigid and prevent the ties from getting crushed.

If you are in a pinch and really need more space, tightly rolling clothing will be the most efficient way to save space. I do this sometimes at the end of a trip if I've bought a few things and need a bit more space to fit it all in. This applies only to non-tailored clothing!

This will give some menswear obsessives a heart attack, but when packing my shoes, I pack only one pair of shoe trees and leave the other pairs empty. I put the trees into whichever pair I've worn each day.

Unless I'm going straight to a meeting after I arrive, I have a very set travel wardrobe comprising

– The Armoury's Army Chino, which is a very full-legged trouser in

a medium-weight cotton. I almost never travel in denim or anything snug. The Armoury's chino is so much more comfortable and I really like the look.

– A Drake's shirt, preferably a tunic-collar model. Drake's classic fit shirts are more generous in the body and go well with The Armoury's chinos.

– A Drake's cardigan or sweater. A bit of knitwear is always useful as an emergency pillow or for cold flights.

– White sneakers by Moonstar; a little-known Japanese sneaker for the domestic market. Essentially a very soft Converse. Sneakers have no metal parts in them, unlike dress shoes (which have an interior metal shank under the arch) so it's one less thing to worry about when going through airport security.

A travel pillow is a must, and the bigger, the better. Human heads are heavy and we lie down at night for a reason: to take the strain off our neck. When you're on a plane, short of lie-down seats in business class, you don't get an opportunity to give your neck a rest, but a neck pillow goes a long way to reduce the strain.

For longer flights, I almost always wear a disposable face mask. Dry sinuses are an additional discomfort that make sleeping on the plane and afterwards more difficult. Wearing a mask helps to keep moisture around the nose and mouth during the flight.

It's very important to stay hydrated. I buy the biggest bottle of water I can at the airport before I get on the plane and I refill it several times during the flight. I try to average around 2 litres of water for a 12-hour flight. It's a bother during the flight but it keeps me from feeling dehydrated after I arrive, making it easier to sleep later. I try to avoid coffee or alcohol right before or during air travel.

Bring a lot of reading material, some of which should be a bit boring and put you to sleep. Use small zip-up pouches to keep various types of carry-on items together and organized while on the plane: one just for passports and SIM cards; one just for power adapters and cables, etc.

It feels good to have a change of scenery. Different parts of the world engage my mind in different ways, so I find thinking on the road quite helpful. The airlines I fly usually don't have WiFi so I get some peace and quiet as well.

I always try to make sure I get some time to eat with local friends while I'm abroad and let them drag me to new places. I rarely tire of the places I'm in – instead I usually wish I could hang around a little longer.

How I Shop When I Travel

Mats Klingberg
Trunk Clothiers, London

Mats is not only the proprietor of one of London's best independent menswear shops – Trunk, in Marylebone – but also one of the best-travelled men around. We asked him for his top tips.

I'm always very interested in discovering new shops and revisiting old ones when I travel, both for myself and to source things for Trunk. I consider myself very lucky to be able to travel and go shopping and still call it work!

When I'm looking for gifts the focus is on the person I'm buying for rather than on myself and/or the shop. But even on these occasions I tend to discover things that might be suitable for Trunk, so it's difficult to keep the two separate. Which isn't necessarily a bad thing.

Discovering something new and interesting always gets me very excited, so when I travel I do my research in advance to make sure I don't miss any obvious places. But I also allow myself to get lost in a city by just walking around in nice areas without paying too much attention to maps. As walking around is essential for

finding new places that aren't already on my radar I prefer to walk as much as possible rather than taking taxis or public transport.

When going to a city for the first time, or one I haven't been to in a while, my main sources of local information are stockist lists, friends and travel guides. Stockist lists for brands that I like are always a good place to start as they tend to list nice stores in nice areas, which are then likely to have other nice stores and restaurants.

Local friends, who know what I like, are another good source of advice, so I always make sure to check in with my network before going somewhere.

Travel guides come in many shapes and forms, so it's important to seek out current ones from sources that you trust, both online and in books

and magazines. The Japanese are very good at finding little hidden gems in cities around the world, so I usually try to get hold of a recent Japanese magazine with travel tips for the city in question. Even if it's all in Japanese (which I don't speak or read!) I can usually tell what's interesting by just looking at the images. Luckily I also have lots of Japanese friends, so when in doubt I just ask someone to translate.

I usually plot all the places of interest on Google maps in order to see where they are in relation to each other and then put together an action plan, making sure to include plenty of nice stops for breakfasts, coffee breaks, lunches, drinks and dinners between the shops.

These are some of my favourite shops around the world:

Any Beams or United Arrows shop in Japan (menswear and accessories)
Japanese buyers always go the extra mile to find nice and interesting things that you haven't seen anywhere else, so it's inspiring to visit Beams and United Arrows, among others, whenever I'm in Japan.

A.GI. EMME in Como (menswear)
A lovely family-run business that has been around for quite some time. They and their customers have essentially grown up together, so they all know each other very well, which creates a very nice atmosphere in the shop. It's well-curated, with a nice mix of everything you need, both smart and casual.

Andreas Murkudis in Berlin (menswear and accessories)
I get space envy with this one! It's a beautiful gallery-like space in a bit of a hidden part of Berlin that you wouldn't stumble upon unless you knew it was there. It has a very well-edited mix of clothing, accessories and nice objects.

Archivando in Tokyo (stationery, homewares)
This is a cute little shop stocked with all sorts of objects that you didn't know you needed until you saw them and felt that you just had to have them! The shop itself has a nice, cosy interior with dimmed lighting.

Svenskt Tenn in Stockholm (interiors)
A bit of a staple in Sweden and the place where lots of wedding gifts come from. Many of its designs were made by Josef Frank in the 1940s, but still feel very relevant today, with lots of bright colours and patterns – so not minimalist at all, which is what most people associate Swedish design with.

Nitty Gritty in Stockholm (menswear)
Located on a residential street in Stockholm's Sodermalm district, this shop is a bit of a destination and always has a good mix of casual contemporary brands. Next door is a great magazine shop also worth visiting.

Daunt Books in London (bookshop)
A must-see for anyone visiting London's Marylebone area, just around the corner from Trunk. It has a great selection of books and I particularly love the section divided into all countries around the world, where you can find traditional travel guides, but also novels and other books from that country.

The Value of Independent Retail

Anda Rowland

Anderson & Sheppard

Anda Rowland has been fighting for independent retail for many years through her work for the Savile Row Bespoke association and groups of independent menswear stores around London, as well as running tailor and haberdasher Anderson & Sheppard. Here she explains why she thinks independent retail is so valuable, and worth the journey to visit in person.

Some brands have lost connection with the shop floor. They treat the customer experience in a shop as secondary, assuming that the sale is a given if the marketing is good enough.

People increasingly miss old-fashioned shopkeeping, where staff are welcoming and knowledgeable, and can talk about the product. It's rare you get that in designer shops or department stores today.

Douglas Hayward, who used to run a wonderful shop and bespoke tailors on Mount Street, would always say 'Know your stock'. You need to know the clothing: why it was made the way it was and how to wear it. Otherwise, why would someone buy from you?

I can see why some shops would think that in-store digital devices are an improvement, but actually it makes things worse. The shop staff become just people who press buttons

on a tablet. Their role is relegated even further. When the staff are doing nothing more than helping to process your order, what's the point in having a shop? It could just be a 'click and collect' service. Is the shop just there for marketing, as a glossy front to the brand?

There's that old quote from Diana Vreeland: 'You're not supposed to give people what they want, you're supposed to give them what they don't know they want yet.' In a proper shop, you might have looked for things online first, but you're open to other ideas, to inspiration. If the curation is any good, you will always find other things that strike you in person, but didn't on a website.

I think it changed after the financial crisis in 2008. Suddenly everyone was re-evaluating what they spent money on. They began asking questions, and

were unwilling to buy something just based on the name.

Today we're in the second wave of that change. People are prepared to spend money, but they want more information. They want to know why something is interesting, valuable, unique. They want to know how and where something was made. They want to make an informed decision.

It's been happening for a while, but fashion brands are consistently behind the curve. You can see the approach changing in technology, for example, where shops and sites increasingly emphasize personal experience and recommendations.

In womenswear the lack of connection to the customer matters less. The drive comes from the creative director and their studio, and if that's successful, that's all that matters.

In menswear, which is less fashion-driven and more about styling and proportion, that model doesn't work. Men want to feel comfortable asking questions, and confident in the responses. And since so much is about colour and texture, the physical experience matters more.

A large part of the appeal in bespoke was always the relationship someone had with their tailor, which involved curation, advice, clothing care and so on. In fact, we've found at the Anderson & Sheppard bespoke shop that there is more and more emphasis on this experience. Given that so few people need to wear a suit every day, commissioning one is more about making the experience interesting, fun, informative. It's the opposite of a purely functional transaction you might have in a high street shop.

It's always going to be a little harder to maintain control and consistency when you have many stores. It is possible when done slowly and organically, but not when you open a dozen stores around the world in one year. The sad thing is that often these stores miss out on a lot of valuable insight from the shopfloor. They see numbers, but they don't see the reasons behind those numbers. Staff will often have no more than an hour's presentation and a PDF to tell them about a new season's product.

Interestingly, as big stores become more transactional and more like an online experience, new online stores are often trying to replicate a physical store experience. Shops like Mr Porter or No Man Walks Alone offer more advice and insight about the product to make up for the fact that they are not seeing the customer in person.

I think that brands are now starting to understand these problems, just a little late. And, of course, independent shops like those in this book are a great reason to be optimistic.

Where and Why I Shop

Wei Koh

Founder, *The Rake*

Wei Koh, the founder of men's luxury magazine *The Rake*, is one of life's nomads. He travels the world for work and pleasure, seeking out the best bars, shops and artisans. Here, he introduces us to a few of his favourite places.

Menswear in particular has grown very fast in recent years, and that has created an issue where you have the same shops selling the same thing in every city, which can be a bit demoralizing.

It has led to the loss of some great stores. One was cutler G. Lorenzi in Milan, which sold some of the finest accessories you could buy, but still had the character of a local store. Via Montenapoleone isn't the same without it.

An example of a shop I love is the jeweller Nardi in Venice. Part of their charm is the fact they are so little known. Back in the 1950s they were considered one of the world's great jewellers, but their profile gradually reduced over the years. Even if I don't go to buy anything, I always visit when I'm in Venice just to get away from all the marketing that surrounds

big jewellery generally. The Venetian style of jewellery is very distinctive, an almost Byzantine combination of Italian and Eastern styles.

I'm a big fan of rock 'n' roll jewellery, and there are some great places around the world: for example, The Great Frog, which is now in the UK and a few US cities; and Crazy Pig Designs in Covent Garden. I've just commissioned a gold skull ring from the latter, in a yellow gold that is the same shade as my vintage Omegas and Rolexes.

I like visiting motorbike shops too, and one of the best is The Bike Shed in London's Old Street. You can buy an amazing motorcycle there, but also great memorabilia. The Real McCoy's probably make the best leather cycle jackets. A Japanese company, with a shop in London, they're obsessive about re-creating old

jackets and styles. And Freewheelers & Co, another Japanese vintage-inspired brand, is also good, and a bit more niche and unusual.

The Japanese are very good at these vintage creations, but I think everyone who ever goes to Tokyo should also visit Ethan Newton's shop, Bryceland's. He's got such extraordinary taste. All the brands are at the highest level of artisanship, but also fit into Ethan's view of the world, which is nicely quirky. He has Liverano and Ambrosi, and even turned me on to an exquisite

hatmaker called Tatton Baird from Springville, Utah.

People talk about going to these shops to experience the place, but for me it's a lot about experiencing the person as well. The shop is really an expression of that person's perspective on the world, and the things in it – the objects they have decided to populate it with.

Simone Righi in Florence is a favourite. He used to run Tie Your Tie but now has his own shop, and I go in there once in a while just because it's such a cool place. I never go with the idea of buying anything specific. I usually just ask Simone, 'What do you think I should purchase? What would suit me?' He'll pick up a tie, or a scarf, and it will be perfect. That's the kind of personal service you can never get online, no matter how well it's curated.

Mariano Rubinacci is good at that too - at picking things out specific to my taste and lifestyle. He will often suggest ties or combinations of ties and pocket squares that I would never think of, but that work immediately. Half the fun is putting yourself in someone else's hands.

I'd include Lino Ieluzzi too, from Al Bazar in Milan. Everyone goes there to hang out with Lino because he's so welcoming. I can't count the number of coffees and conversations I've had with Lino over the years, yet I'm convinced he doesn't speak any English! I always leave with something small - it's the best souvenir.

Other places I'd include would be Marinella in Naples. So small and basic, but it's lovely talking to Maurizio [Marinella]. And Charvet in Paris. Whether you like their style or not, it's always worth a visit.

As a man you have a vision of yourself, what you like to wear and how you want to come across. You have to trust the person helping you do that, whether it's a tailor, a shoemaker or a curator in a shop. Trust is key, and it's a very delicate thing. Each time they recommend something, or make something, it will reinforce that trust or damage it.

I think the thing to remember is that the very act of shopping is unnecessary. None of us need these things; any essentials can be acquired quickly and easily online. The act of shopping is all about the experience, from beginning to end. That is what will keep all these independent stores going in the long run.

Florence

In addition to its well-known tourist destinations – the Uffizi Gallery, the Piazza del Duomo, the Ponte Vecchio – Florence is famous as a menswear hub, especially in January and June, when it plays host to the men's fashion trade show Pitti Uomo. But the city has enough unique shops to make it worth a visit for the sartorial traveller at any time of the year. Florence has always had a large population of artisans, particularly for paper and leather goods, and some of Italy's best tailors and shoemakers reside there today.

The List

1 Sartoria Vestrucci

www.sartoriavestrucci.com
Via Maggio 58R, 50125

See Brand Focus on pages 32–37.

2 Simone Abbarchi

simoneabbarchi.com
Borgo Santissimi Apostoli 16, 50123

See Brand Focus on pages 38–41.

3 Scuola del Cuoio

www.scuoladelcuoio.com
Via S. Giuseppe 5, 50122

See Brand Focus on pages 42–45.

4 Santa Maria Novella

www.smnovella.com
Via della Scala 16, 50123

The perfumery Santa Maria Novella has a case for being the most beautiful shop in the world. Founded by the church's Dominican monks in the 17th century, it sits in its own magnificent section of the basilica, complete with ornate frescoes and paintings charting the history of the family. There is a selection of fragrances, shaving creams and other products for men, alongside women's scents, liqueurs and home fragrances. Although the firm's products are now made off-site and stocked in stores around the world, its original home in the basilica is a shop like no other and must be experienced firsthand.

5 Liverano & Liverano

liverano.com
Via dei Fossi 43, 50123

Florence's best-known bespoke tailor cuts in a flattering and surprisingly modern style with a slightly shorter jacket, rounded fronts and wide lapels. Although expensive, the work is first-rate. The shop has a collection of vintage fabric bolts, which are always nice to drape across the body when picking out a suit, as well as some ready-to-wear garments and accessories.

6 Stefano Bemer

stefanobemer.com
Via di S. Niccolò 2, 50125

Since Stefano's sad passing, his shoemaking company has been taken over by Tommaso Melani (of the family behind Scuola del Cuoio) and moved to a beautiful old church on the south side of the Arno. There, the customer can pick from ready-made, made-to-order and bespoke shoes – while the craftsmen all work in view around the ground floor. A shoemaking school runs on the top floor.

1

7 Lorenzo Villoresi

www.lorenzovilloresi.it
Via de' Bardi 12, 50125

Florence has a strong reputation for
artisan perfumers, and just down the
road from Stefano Bemer is the relatively
new shop attached to Lorenzo Villoresi's
studio. Lorenzo creates unique perfumes
with intensity and character that come
in beautiful blue-glass bottles. Most of
the fragrances are unisex, but Acqua di
Colonia is a particularly nice take on the
classic male cologne.

8 Il Micio

Via de' Federighi 6, 50123

Over the years many Japanese artisans
have come to Florence, often training
as shoemakers before returning to their
home country. One who has stayed and
carved out his own local reputation is
Hidetaka Fukaya, known as 'Il Micio'
(The Cat). His bespoke shoes are very
finely made and tend to have the
elongated silhouette favoured by many
Japanese makers. There is also a small
range of leather goods.

9 Frasi

www.simonerighi.it
Via de' Federighi 7, 50123

Just down the street from Hidetaka is the menswear store Frasi, run by Simone Righi. The dapper, bearded Simone has acquired quite a cult following among menswear enthusiasts in recent years, initially after featuring on street-style blog The Sartorialist. His shop offers an eclectic mix of accessories and tailoring, with an emphasis on colour and pattern.

10 Sartoria Corcos

www.sartoriacorcos.com
Via della Vigna Nuova 26, 50123

Also nearby is Sartoria Corcos, the first-floor workshop of Japanese tailor Kotaro Miyahira. Kotaro is a young tailor who has gathered a strong clientele, attracted by both his relatively low prices and his strong style – which combines classic Florentine elements with broader influences. At the time of writing, however, he was not taking on any new clients.

3

11 Ugolini

www.roberto-ugolini.com
Via dei Michelozzi 17, 50125

The best-known Florentine shoemaker apart from Stefano Bemer is Ugolini. Located on the south side of the river on Via dei Michelozzi, the workshop offers only bespoke. A good range of bespoke designs can be seen on the website.

12 Mannina

www.manninafirenze.com
Via de' Guicciardini 16, 50125

A third shoemaker worth investigating, particularly on value for money, is Mannina, founded by Calogero Mannina in 1953 and now run by his son Antonio. His boots and spectator models are especially popular.

13 Bernardo

www.bernardofirenze.it
Via Porta Rossa 87, 50123

There are fewer multi-brand menswear stores in Florence than in Milan and Rome, but the stand-out is Bernardo. Although small, it has a well-curated selection of clothing from the likes of Aspesi, Incotex, Herno and Fedeli – all brands that have long been favourites in Italy, but have only recently gained a following elsewhere in the world.

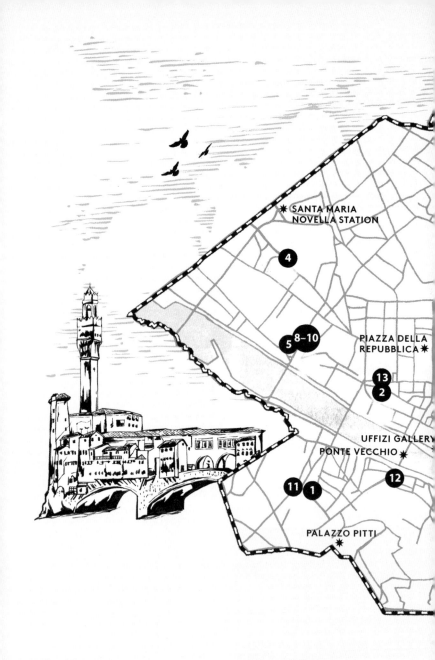

SANTA MARIA
NOVELLA STATION

4

8-10

5

PIAZZA DELLA
REPUBBLICA

13
2

UFFIZI GALLERY
PONTE VECCHIO

12

11 1

PALAZZO PITTI

Florence

UOMO

SAN NICCOLO

Sartoria Vestrucci

A new shop with an old reputation, Sartoria Vestrucci is setting out to spread the word about Florentine tailoring around the world

In 2017 several interesting new menswear shops opened in Florence, including the reborn Tie Your Tie. But perhaps the biggest was Sartoria Vestrucci, the tailoring house led by Tommaso Melani of Stefano Bemer.

The Vestrucci shop is on the south side of the Arno in Florence, with a small entrance that leads to a deep space, running back through racks of ready-made tailoring to cutting tables for bespoke garments at the rear.

At the first table stands venerable Loris Vestrucci, already once-retired, smiling and cheeky, picking apart basting stitches and muttering his views on any tailoring within his view. Behind him work two apprentices, hired for him to train and provide some future for the bespoke.

The style will be familiar to anyone aware of the peculiarities of Florentine tailoring. The shoulder of the jacket is a little extended, but only lightly padded, with a fairly natural run down into the sleeve. Its width creates an impression of strength without requiring heavy padding or roping. The chest is cut clean without being too close, and is accentuated by broad lapels. Like most Tuscan jackets, it has no front seam running down below the hip pocket.

One difference from the style of other Florentine tailors (most obviously Liverano & Liverano) is that the lapel is straighter rather than obviously concave. The front quarters are also relatively closed.

The double-breasted jacket has a fairly low and flat gorge. This is more in fashion now after years of high, pointy lapels that threatened to flop down the back of the jacket.

OPPOSITE Shoes – and chair! – made by actor Daniel Day-Lewis.

RIGHT Basted Vestrucci jacket on display.

BELOW Fitting for a grey flannel suit with Loris Vestrucci (centre).

PAGE 32 A finished Vestrucci jacket, with colourful accessories.

OVERLEAF The Vestrucci showroom, with tailoring at the back of the shop.

One of the reasons Tommaso Melani says he was excited about launching Vestrucci was that the distinctive Florentine style is under-represented in the ready-made market, and that's certainly true: Italian tailoring around the world is currently dominated by Naples and the Abruzzo region.

The quality of work in a bespoke Vestrucci jacket is very high, and a challenge of the new brand has been to reflect this level of tailoring in the ready-to-wear line. They've largely succeeded, with neat finishing and most of the Vestrucci style details apparent in the jackets. This does make the prices quite high – around €3000 including VAT for a ready-made suit, and a little more for made-to-order. Bespoke starts at €6000 including VAT.

Vestrucci now does trunk shows in partnership with Stefano Bemer in London, New York and elsewhere. This enables customers to have bespoke or ready-to-wear shoes, trousers and suits from the same group.

In the meantime, I highly recommend visiting the Vestrucci shop in Florence. It doesn't have the character of an older tailoring boutique, but there is an excellent range of ready-to-wear on display to try on, along with Bemer shoes, a nice selection of knitted ties and leather goods.

Simone Abbarchi

A combination of value and style make Simone Abbarchi
a popular local shirtmaker in Florence – as well as on
his travels to London and New York

Simone Abbarchi is a Florence-based shirtmaker with a small shop in the centre of town. His shirts strike a good balance between reasonable price and high quality. Made-to-measure shirts start at €120, with a more involved bespoke offering at €150. Given that this is the price of many designer ready-made shirts, it is not surprising that he has developed such a strong local following.

Simone's shirts are of course also made to specific measurements, so the fit is a lot better, and they have the distinctive Italian collar construction: a lightly fused lining that curls around the collar of a jacket when the neck is undone, yet sits crisply with a tie when the collar is fastened. This stiffness usually requires the use of collar bones – although if you prefer to go without collar bones you can also have the

'sprezzatura' look of a collar that curls at the corner, perhaps nonchalantly outside of the jacket lapel.

One reason Simone's shirts are so reasonable is they have almost no handwork. The buttons are sewn on by hand, but that's it. Personally I prefer a hand-attached collar and sleeve, but you pay more for that.

The made-to-measure offering involves no paper pattern, and you should expect small aspects of the fit not to be as good as bespoke (as with all made-to-measure, it's about 2D changes rather than the 3D approach you get with bespoke). But this is far less important on shirts than on other types of tailoring.

Simone's bespoke, as with other makers, does involve creating a pattern, followed by a fitting on a partially made shirt. This may not

THIS PAGE AND OPPOSITE ABOVE Finished shirts, accessories, fabrics and collar options on display.

OPPOSITE BELOW Interior of the Simone Abbarchi shop in Florence.

be practical if your visit to Florence is short, though Simone (and assistant Gianluca Cocchetti) also visits London and New York twice a year – February and September for London, and March and October for New York. He doesn't have a minimum for an order, and will usually do two fittings for a first shirt, but can just do one if the customer accepts that there might be tiny things to change next time. His made-to-measure shirts, however, are usually finished more quickly and sent straight to the customer.

For anyone just getting into bespoke and made-to-measure shirts, Simone is a great choice.

PAGE 38 A wing collar made by Simone Abbarchi for evening wear.

Florence

42

Scuola del Cuoio

With workshops and a school in an old monastery – but still right in the centre of the city – Scuola del Cuoio is worth a visit as much for its history as for its bags and accessories

Traditional Florentine leather manufacturer Scuola del Cuoio was founded in 1950 by Franciscan monks of the monastery of Santa Croce to provide training and employment for local orphans of the Second World War. The monks partnered with the Gori and Casini families, who had been in the leather business since the 1930s. Three sisters from the Gori family – Laura, Francesca and Barbara – run Scuola del Cuoio today, along with Laura's son Tommaso Melani, who also runs Sartoria Vestrucci and Stefano Bemer shoes in the city.

The monastery's old dormitories were used to house the orphans, and workbenches were placed in the corridor outside – hence the slightly odd set-up today, where most of the work is done on long benches in (admittedly, rather ornate) corridors.

The school and workshop now has twelve full-time workers plus three teachers, who work with twenty students in larger premises downstairs (the 13th-century stables). Although the school is tucked under and between the various rooms of the monastery, it is a spectacular setting – truly part of the ancient basilica.

Students have placements of three or six months, during which they learn most aspects of making bags and small leather goods. They are trained in basic leather-working techniques including cutting (everything is cut by hand) and machine- and hand-stitching, as well as more specialized skills such as weaving leather. Laura Gori is keen to point out that intrecciato leather weaving is a traditional house technique that has been practised for decades.

ABOVE AND PAGE 42 The Santa Croce monastery has to be one of the most picturesque workshop settings in the world.

OPPOSITE The wide range of bags and leather accessories made at Scuola del Cuoio.

The students often go on to positions in the menswear industry. One graduate recently joined the quality-control division at Ralph Lauren.

Most of the production – around 70% – is of women's bags, but the workshop also makes a few bags and accessories for men, including elegant belts, wallets, briefcases and messenger bags. Its leather desk sets are rather famous, as an early connection with the US Army led to President Dwight D. Eisenhower commissioning a leather set for the desk of the Oval Office. American presidents up until Bill Clinton continued this tradition.

The school's products are also sold online and in the Four Seasons Hotel in Florence but the on-site Scuola del Cuoio shop is worth a visit in person. Bespoke bags are available and are especially popular with American and Arab customers who appreciate the brightly coloured, jewelled and embroidered creations that are made to order or as one-off designs by Laura's sister Francesca.

Among all the wonderful places to see in Florence, Scuola del Cuoio is worth visiting for the setting and the history – following in the footsteps of past visitors including Princess Diana, Katharine Hepburn, Cary Grant and Ted Kennedy.

Hong Kong

Hong Kong has long been a centre for international commerce, driven by its location as a key port and later by its strategic importance to the British Empire. When it was handed back to China in 1997, the city retained its vibrancy and international flavour, due to that heritage and the success of its financial markets. Chinese from the mainland came for tax-free Western goods, leading to a plethora of designer brands and watch shops, but there was little in menswear with its own identity. That began to change in the 2010s with the opening of independent shops such as The Armoury, whose style has become influential around the world. With this new generation of shops, and a revival of interest in local bespoke tailors such as W. W. Chan, Hong Kong is now emerging as a strong menswear destination in Asia.

The List

1 The Armoury

TheArmoury.com
**1a 307 Pedder Building,
  12 Pedder Street, Central
1b B47 Landmark Central,
  15 Queen's Road, Central**

See the Brand Focus on pages 54–59.

The Armoury has two stores in Hong Kong. The smaller one at 12 Pedder Street is the cosiest, and tends to host the trunk shows by visiting bespoke tailors, shoemakers and other artisans. If you're interested in bespoke, it's worth visiting here first, where you will get the inside line on artisans and the details on other speciality pieces in-store. If you're new to The Armoury, however, and perhaps also to many of the brands it carries, then start in the larger store in the lower ground floor of Landmark Central, just across the street.

2 Bryceland's Co

www.brycelandsco.com
**7/F, Luk Yu Building,
  24–26 Stanley Street, Central**

The Hong Kong branch of Ethan Newton's sartorial/workwear store has a different atmosphere to the original in Tokyo, and features a good selection of local pieces, such as trousers made with W. W. Chan. See the Brand Focus on the Tokyo branch on pages 204–07 for more on Bryceland's.

3 Attire House

attire-house.com
**4/F, Duke Wellington House,
  14–24 Wellington Street, Central**

When Attire House opened in Hong Kong, with a similar inspiration to The Armoury, its most obvious point of difference was the lifestyle additions: a cocktail bar (run by Japan's Bar High Five) and a barbershop (from Korean company Herr) alongside the menswear. They also quickly had some of the biggest names in bespoke menswear doing their trunk shows at the store, including tailors Anderson & Sheppard from London, shoemaker Marquess from Tokyo and tailors Solito from Naples. In 2018 the House moved to a new location around the corner, abandoning the bar (always a little separate, on the floor above) but adding a cigar lounge. The feel is now more laid back, and there is

1

room for the stock such as shoes from Alden, Crockett & Jones and Edward Green, and accessories from Albert Thurston, Postalco and E. Marinella.

4 W. W. Chan & Sons

wwchan.com

Unit B, 8/F, Entertainment Building, 30 Queen's Road Central, Central

Hong Kong is famous for its tailors – but largely of the wrong sort. Shops and hawkers will offer a bespoke suit in 24 hours at very low prices, but the quality can be low, with square cuts and a poor fit. It's usually best to stick to more established names, and to accept the standard bespoke process of multiple fittings over a period of weeks. One of the best in the city is W. W. Chan, which has been in operation since 1952. It descends from the original 'Red Gang' of tailors from Shanghai, but has consistently refined and updated its styles over the years, unlike many such traditional houses. If your stay in Hong Kong is too short for bespoke fittings W. W. Chan also regularly travels to the USA, Australia and Europe.

5 Ascot Chang

www.ascotchang.com

Four Hong Kong locations including:

5a Shop 2031, Podium Level 2 of IFC Mall, 1 Harbour View Street, Central

5b MW6, Peninsula Hotel, Salisbury Road, Hong Kong

As with suits, so with shirts. Any cheap tailor in Hong Kong will offer to chuck in a few shirts to sweeten the deal, but there are very few quality bespoke

shirtmakers around. Ascot Chang, however, is one of them. Its founder trained in Shanghai before setting up shop in Hong Kong in 1949, originally selling shirts to businessmen door-to-door. Today the company has stores in the USA, China and the Philippines, largely run by Chang's apprentices and offering bespoke shirts whose measurements have to be communicated to the Hong Kong headquarters via a complex note-taking system; it also holds regular trunk shows in Japan, Europe and the Middle East. But it's worth visiting one of the Hong Kong locations for a slice of local Chinese craft history.

6 Drop93

Drop93.com

B01, 6th Floor, Cheung Lung Industrial Building, 10 Cheung Yee Street, Lai Chi Kok, Kowloon

Drop93 is a retail concept launched by The Armoury, aiming to find new homes for clothing no longer worn by its customers, or for spare pieces made by other brands. Most of Drop93's sales activity is online, offering a wide range of tailoring, shoes and accessories, sometimes in multiple sizes. But there is also a physical showroom outside the centre of Hong Kong in Lai Chi Kok, where anyone interested in pieces on the site can go to try them on in person.

7 Prologue

www.prologuehk.com

3 Shin Hing Street, Central

Prologue is one of the newest classically minded independent menswear stores

1

to set up in Hong Kong. It offers more unusual visiting artisans, such as Japanese shoemakers Clematis and Bolero, and its own line of tailoring. This tailoring draws heavily on the styles of the founders' favourite Italian makers, particularly from Florence and Naples, and all the work is done locally. The shop is a little tucked away, a move that was intended to make it feel more like a tailoring atelier. It also stocks brands such as Mementomori accessories and Yanko shoes.

8 Tassels
www.tassels.com.hk
8a Shop B64-65, The Landmark, Central
8b 6th Floor, SOGO Causeway Bay Store, 555 Hennessy Road, Causeway Bay

A classic men's shoe store, Tassels stocks English brands such as Crockett & Jones, Edward Green and Cheaney; Alden from the USA; and accessories by E. Marinella, among others. There are two branches in Hong Kong, in the Central and Causeway Bay areas, and one in Beijing. The Hong Kong shops host regular trunk shows with made-to-order offerings.

9 Take5
www.take5jeans.com
1/F 17 Cameron Road, Tsim Sha Tsui

Take5 is a mecca for denim in Hong Kong, stocking a huge range of Japanese brands. Although not easy to find (it's on an upper floor) and not necessarily sartorial in style, it is worth a trip purely for its fantastic wall-of-denim display. Alongside names such as Iron Heart, Momotaro and The Flat Head are several collaborations Take5 has done with different makers, and a range of leather jackets.

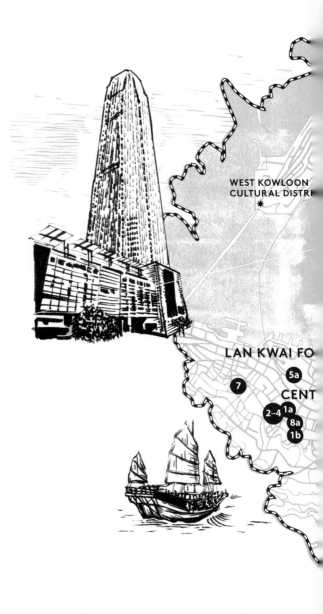

WEST KOWLOON
CULTURAL DISTRI

LAN KWAI FO

5a

7

CENT

2–4 1a

8a

1b

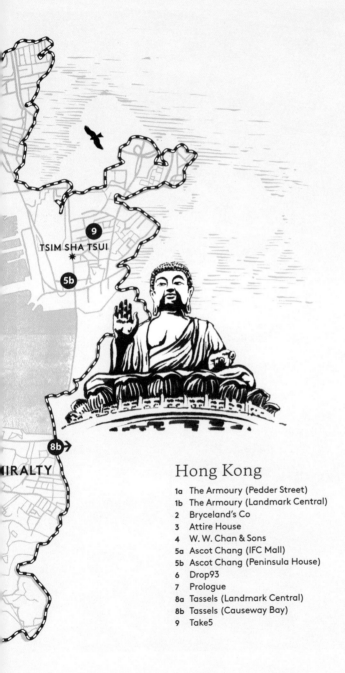

TSIM SHA TSUI

Hong Kong

1a The Armoury (Pedder Street)
1b The Armoury (Landmark Central)
2   Bryceland's Co
3   Attire House
4   W. W. Chan & Sons
5a Ascot Chang (IFC Mall)
5b Ascot Chang (Peninsula House)
6   Drop93
7   Prologue
8a Tassels (Landmark Central)
8b Tassels (Causeway Bay)
9   Take5

The Armoury

The Armoury offers a closely curated range of classic menswear with a distinctive Hong Kong identity and personal approach to selection, even though many brands promoted by Mark, Alan and the team have now become well-known

Hong Kong's sartorial menswear scene, previously dominated by international luxury brands, began to develop its own identity in 2010 when Alan See, Mark Cho and Ethan Newton opened The Armoury: a small store on the first floor of a building in Pedder Street specializing in fine tailoring and European brands with a heritage of craft. The Armoury's influence was felt not just in Hong Kong, but around the world, and has inspired shops as far abroad as Toronto and Tokyo, as well as a new generation of other independent menswear stores in Hong Kong. There are now two branches of The Armoury in Hong Kong (and one in New York).

The Armoury specializes in classic menswear – suits, shirts, ties – from some of the finest makers around the world. It introduced men to the likes of Japanese artisan bag-maker Ortus, who visits for bespoke trunk shows, and popularized shoemakers such as Saint Crispin's from Romania, and Carmina from Mallorca.

The reason it stands above so many other classic clothing stores, however, is the quality of its customer service and house style. Founders Mark Cho and Alan See wanted to reproduce in The Armoury the relationships they had with their own bespoke tailors in Hong Kong and in Europe. So: great interpersonal customer service, and knowledge of a wide range of goods to enable men to build a complete modern wardrobe.

That wardrobe would also be stylish. Mark, Alan and former business partners Ethan Newton and Jake Grantham made tailoring seem fresh and young, with soft-shouldered

PAGE 54 The range of Armoury accessories is impressive, from loafers to watch rolls.

OPPOSITE Knowledgeable customer service and the taste with which it styles its artisan pieces are the foundations of The Armoury's success.

OVERLEAF The larger Landmark branch.

jackets, free-flowing ties and casual outerwear. Much of it, they would admit, came straight from Italy, but no one had made the style so accessible before – in Hong Kong or elsewhere – or made such effective use of social media to spread it around the world.

Today the mix of brands has changed and expanded, but the feel is just the same. Alongside long-standing Neapolitan partner Salvatore Ambrosi, (see page 117) who makes some of the finest bespoke trousers in the world, is Japanese manufacturer Ring Jacket (see page 201), whose tailoring the staff of The Armoury have adapted to their own styles and models.

The store launched its own shoe range in 2017 (with lasts designed by Japanese shoemaker Yohei Fukuda) but it still also stocks other brands including Carmina. Additional craft manufacturers brought to prominence by the store over the years include Japanese glasses-maker Nackymade and American leather-goods maker Frank Clegg. Outerwear brand Coherence is another recent example of a maker that has been popularized by the store and offers something genuinely different in its original fabrics and cuts.

'All our artisans are united by a commitment to craft and to traditional aspects of style,' says See. 'Ortus, for example, is a bespoke leather-goods maker who sews every part of his bags by hand – and even makes his own hardware. He makes a handful of ready-made pieces every year exclusively for us.' Other bespoke artisans who, like Ortus, visit for trunk shows include tailors Liverano & Liverano from Florence (see page 27), Musella Dembech from Milan (see page 97), and Ciccio from Tokyo (see pages 214–15).

These bespoke visits tend to take place in the smaller, more intimate store on Pedder Street, while the second Armoury store across the road in the Landmark building is larger and stocks a wider range of products. Both are worth a visit. Not only was The Armoury the original among the next generation of Hong Kong menswear stores, but it also remains one of the city's most innovative.

It's worth noting that the Armoury-branded products are often some of the best, combining Mark and Alan's impeccable taste with their wide knowledge of manufacturers. Try their in-house polo shirts, which are one of the few polo models to work well under tailoring, and the workwear-inspired chinos.

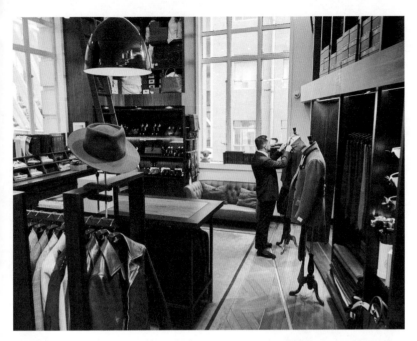

London

London is best known as the home of traditional bespoke tailoring – on Savile Row – and many of the 20th century's biggest fashion crazes were also born here, often alongside the emergence of new music. London used to have a strong menswear retail scene, but in the 1980s and 1990s this fell away, with independent shops losing out to department stores and big designer brands. Such stores remained open across Germany and Italy long after they had closed in the UK.

The past 20 years, however, have been a story of London's renaissance, in luxury menswear in particular. As Savile Row has started to regain its vigour, so too has the retail scene, with the opening of new menswear boutiques offering a variety of takes on elegant style. London has far too many great shops to mention all of them individually. Some are therefore grouped together by type, such as the tailors, and others mentioned only in passing. There is plenty to explore, in a city easy to browse on foot.

The List

1 Dege & Skinner
dege-skinner.co.uk
10 Savile Row, W1S 3PJ

See Brand Focus on pages 68–71.

2 Connolly
connollyengland.com
4 Clifford Street, W1S 2LG

See Brand Focus on pages 72–75.

3 Anderson & Sheppard Haberdashery
www.anderson-sheppard.co.uk/
 haberdashery
17 Clifford Street, W1S 3RQ

See Brand Focus on pages 76–81.

4 Trunk Clothiers
www.trunkclothiers.com
8 Chiltern Street, W1U 7PU

5 Trunk Labs
34 Chiltern Street, W1U 7QH

A trailblazer when it first opened, stocking Incotex trousers, Boglioli jackets and Common Projects trainers, Trunk Clothiers is still the best shop in London for quality casual clothing with a classic aesthetic. Trunk Labs, a sister shop on the same street, stocks luggage, footwear and homewares.

6 Drake's
www.drakes.com
3 Clifford Street, W1S 2LF

With a strong aesthetic and a growing reach, the famed British tiemaker's first shop offers a lot more than ties. Favourites include their shawl-collar sweater, nicely styled jackets and a new, strong shirt offering. In recent seasons Drake's has also expanded into footwear and outerwear.

7 Gaziano & Girling
www.gazianogirling.com
39 Savile Row, W1S 3QF

8 George Cleverley
www.georgecleverley.com
13 The Royal Arcade, W1S 4SL

9 John Lobb
www.johnlobbltd.co.uk
9 St James's Street, SW1A 1EF

These are the only dedicated shops in the world for each of these top-end shoemakers. All three are worth a visit: Gaziano & Girling for its range of bespoke and ready-made shoes, and its superb patination; Cleverley for its workshops upstairs; and John Lobb for the rabbit-warren nature of the place. Few other shoe shops in the world are so interesting as these.

3

1

10 Henry Poole

henrypoole.com
15 Savile Row, W1S 3PJ

11 Chittleborough & Morgan

www.chittleboroughandmorgan.co.uk
12 Savile Row, W1S 3PQ

12 Anderson & Sheppard Bespoke

www.anderson-sheppard.co.uk
32 Old Burlington Street, W1S 3AT

There are perhaps a dozen bespoke tailors in central London who are worth visiting. You're unlikely to have time to visit them all, and they are not really shops for extended browsing – you go in for a polite inquiry, and perhaps an explanation of house style. Most are pretty welcoming, however. If you're looking to commission a suit, pick out a few likely candidates. If you're more interested in a taste of tailoring history, visit the likes of Henry Poole, Gieves & Hawkes and Huntsman.

13 Private White V.C.

www.privatewhitevc.com
73 Duke Street, W1K 5NP

This long-running British manufacturer set up its own menswear line a few years ago, offering well-made jackets and coats at very reasonable prices. The pieces are distinguished by the functional aspects of their designs, by touches of copper hardware and by a very open pricing policy.

14 Lock & Co.

www.lockhatters.co.uk
6 St James's Street, SW1A 1EF

15 Bate's

www.bates-hats.co.uk
73 Jermyn Street, SW1Y 6NP

16 Christy's

www.christys-hats.com
12 Princes Arcade, SW1Y 6DS

Nowhere else in the world would you find three great hat companies in such close proximity. Lock & Co. has the most history, of course, and beautiful hatboxes, but if you're actually shopping for a hat then the other two are worth visiting as well.

17 Nigel Cabourn
www.cabourn.com
28 Henrietta Street, WC2E 8NA

18 The Real McCoy's
www.realmccoyslondon.com
15 Henrietta Street, WC2E 8QG

These two casualwear brands both set up their first shops in London a few years ago, on opposite sides of the street. Both specialize in re-creations of old styles, with Japanese outfit McCoy's aiming for precise imitations, and British brand Cabourn more inspiration and modern improvement. The latter also does more seasonal designs, and the coats and knitwear are especially recommended. This is Cabourn's flagship shop and McCoy's only one outside Japan.

19 Son of a Stag
www.sonofastag.com
9 Dray Walk, E1 6QL

This is possibly the best shop in London for denim and leather, with stacks of imported Japanese brands, leather jackets from around the world and chain-stitching done on site. If you like the workwear style, it's also worth checking out Present and Blackhorse Lane Ateliers in this area of east London.

20 Turnbull & Asser
www.turnbullandasser.co.uk
71–72 Jermyn Street, SW1Y 6PF

The sheer scale of the Jermyn Street flagship shop will impress most people. Quality menswear and accessories of almost every conceivable sort are on offer with bespoke around the corner in the same building. Although it is getting more of a designer edge of late, it is still one of the broadest offerings for sartorial men in London.

21 New & Lingwood
www.newandlingwood.com
53 Jermyn Street, SW1Y 6LX

Across the street from Turnbull & Asser is another unique outfitter spread across two shops. New & Lingwood is recommended for men with more unusual tastes in both colour and design. Few other places stock cloaks. Few have so much in green and pink. Plus the dressing gowns are beautiful.

22 Bentley's Antiques
bentleyslondon.com
91 Lower Sloane Street, SW1W 8DA

This lovely antiques store specializes in luggage, bags and men's accessories, with a well-curated and revolving collection. It is particularly good for sought-after trunks from the likes of Louis Vuitton and Goyard.

MARYLEBONE

OXFORD STREET

MARBLE ARCH

MAYFAIR

BUCKINGHAM PALACE

VENT GARDEN

7
18

✳ **LONDON EYE**

BEN

19

London

Dege & Skinner

A tour of the storied Savile Row tailor
reveals a wealth of military regalia
as well as civilian tailoring

Dege & Skinner have never been ones to blow their own trumpet. But in the past few years there have been small signs of the 150-year-old, family-run tailor stepping out into the spotlight.

In 2012 the firm took over the workrooms under its shop on Savile Row, allowing more tailoring staff to work on site. In 2015 there were some lovely celebrations for their century-and-a-half anniversary. And in 2016 they began offering ready-to-wear suiting for the first time, making their style more accessible to those on a smaller budget. 'We get so much foot traffic – partly because we don't have the imposing staircase of the other firms,' explains front-of-house Matthew Cowley of the shop's appeal to visitors, 'And while they don't want bespoke, they want something with the Dege look and feel.'

The ready-to-wear line is a pretty conservative selection of navy and grey suits, and navy blazers, with the suits starting at £950. 'It is certainly our style – we tweaked the shape and moved the buttons and pockets a touch,' says Cowley. 'Plus we do all the alterations in-house, so you get that tailoring expertise.' That last point is where tailors on the Row often set themselves apart from high street stores selling ready-to-wear suits.

So what is the Dege & Skinner house style?

It is a fairly strong-shouldered, structured look, similar to that of other Savile Row tailors such as Huntsman and Richard Anderson. Unlike those houses, however, Dege & Skinner doesn't do many one-button jackets, preferring to keep that style for dinner suits. Most of its single-breasted jackets are two-button, with a 'true' (no roll) three-button style for more casual, country pieces.

The lapel usually has a subtle curve. There is little rope to the shoulder, and not much drape in the chest or flare to the skirt. The cuffs normally have two working and two show buttonholes. Dege's overall look is clean and close, much influenced by the range of military tailoring the house does (which all the cutters are trained in).

That military tailoring is everywhere around the shop. It catches your eye on the mannequins, and jumps out when you start looking through the racks of fittings waiting downstairs.

There's the mess dress of the Royal Lancers, with its beautiful embroidery and cape-like jacket. The buttons down the front are used to disguise a zip – if you see one without the buttons, the piece has to be slipped over the head and zipped up at the side or back instead.

This uniform was designed by Dege & Skinner for a new cavalry regiment. As the number of British cavalry units decreases, historic units are being merged, requiring a new dress uniform that incorporates aspects of each unit's traditional dress. Another great piece is a rich purple mess jacket and vest for the Royal Hussars. It is similar in design to the Royal Lancers' jacket but with that zip fastening up the back. Some Dege customers apply some of these military points to their civilian tailoring: one recently ordered a frock coat with embroidery up the arms, to wear on his motorcycle.

ABOVE The mess dress of the Royal Lancers.

LEFT AND RIGHT Core to the skill of bespoke is creating a unique paper pattern for each customer, whether for shirts (left) or suits (right).

RIGHT The storied Dege & Skinner shop on Savile Row.

BELOW Frogging detail on a bespoke dinner jacket.

BELOW RIGHT The classic two-button Dege & Skinner jacket.

PAGE 68 A linen jacket awaiting a fitting.

Military tailoring still makes up about 30% of Dege's work. Its tailors travel every week to Sandhurst to outfit new officers, and made the uniforms for princes William and Harry when they were commissioned into the Blues & Royals.

The newly acquired workroom downstairs is bright and roomy, with just a few touches of personality starting to creep onto the walls around the apprentices and trouser-makers. This is often the nicest part of visiting a workshop: seeing the family photos, the pin-ups, the cheery reminders that 'You don't have to be mad to work here – but it helps!' that build up naturally over time, like limpets decorating a rock.

The apprentices working downstairs are a welcome sight, as you watch them repeatedly practising traditional techniques, such as hand-padding a piece of canvas, in order to master them. Their presence suggests a strong future for Dege, as well as an illustrious past.

Connolly

The reborn Connolly manages to combine the best of luxury menswear and original design, on what is becoming the best location for men's retail in London: Clifford Street

Connolly, which re-opened on Clifford Street in 2016, is one of the most interesting menswear stores in London. It offers luxury clothing under its own name, as well as a few European brands (Charvet, Car Shoe, Stile Latino), covering everything from knitwear to tailoring, shoes and leather goods.

It is best understood, however, as three different collections: the Driving Collection, the Classic Collection and the leather goods. Each has a distinctive look, and seeing just one (for example, by not visiting the lower-ground floor) could mean missing out on what is a very rich and original contribution to menswear.

The first, and most accessible, is the Driving Collection. It is a mix of knitwear, soft tailoring, outerwear and accessories, all beautifully made

and offering good value by luxury standards, often with small and original design quirks. A cashmere knitted jacket, for example, has piped seams and is slightly felted to give it a little more of the feel and drape of cloth. Or a cream-canvas tote with the most subtle white leather binding.

There aren't many pieces in each category of the Driving Collection. This is not where you go to fill up on navy ties or pale blue shirts. But each piece has an interesting aesthetic without becoming too fashion-y. The key summer shirt might be a broad blue-and-cream stripe in a linen/cotton mix, with a relaxed cut. Next to it might be a herringbone linen jacket, wonderfully slubby and softly structured.

The Classic Collection is a different kettle of fish. Designed by

Marc Audibet – of Hermès, Prada, Ferragamo and others – it is more fashion-forward, featuring unusual cuts, materials and proportions. The colour palette, however, is still very restrained (mostly navy, cream and brown), which keeps the pieces relevant for most men. An oversized ribbed cream sweater, for example, is identical in colour, knit and materials to a classic piece we'd expect from a traditional Scottish knitter – but the neck is scooped and high, and the body is voluminous, high in the waist and then expanding in the chest. And the cuff is very long: two or three times the length of a classic piece. None of these design points are extreme. This is not a showy piece of fashion (you'd struggle to pick it out coming down a runway). But the overall effect is very distinctive.

Some pieces in the Classic Collection are less unusual: a beige suede safari jacket, for instance. Others – such as the floor-length *liquette* overshirts that make an interesting dressing-gown substitute – are much more so.

But there are always pieces at a perfect, wearable point in the middle: for example, knitted polo shirts in cream with navy ribbing (or navy with cream) that have extended sleeves finishing just above the elbow. All of the pieces in the Classic Collection also have nice manufacturing details: the full-length pleats in the *liquette*, or a strip of herringbone knitting before the edge of the cuff in the polo shirts.

Founded in 1879, Connolly was originally a leather business that made the interiors for some of the world's best-known cars as well as for the British Houses of Parliament. Its clothing shop opened in 1995, in a crescent just off Belgrave Square. Founder Isabel Ettedgui was responsible for bringing many luxury brands to London for the first time, including Charvet and Car Shoe.

It was the best curated luxury shop in the city, and had a real loyalty among men in Mayfair, as well as a great clubby atmosphere. It expanded and moved to Conduit Street in 2000, before closing in 2010 with the death of Isabel's husband (and founder of Joseph), Joseph Ettedgui. Eight years later, it's reinvigorating menswear once more.

ABOVE The range at Connolly includes vintage leather, sportswear and beachwear as well as more everyday pieces.

OPPOSITE The shop is one of the most attractive in London, occupying an entire house on Clifford Street in Mayfair.

PAGE 72 An oversized and indulgent cashmere cardigan.

Anderson & Sheppard Haberdashery

By taking a fresh look at the cuts and colours
of traditional menswear, the Haberdashery
has brought a unique shop to Mayfair

Anderson & Sheppard, the Savile Row tailor whose history of bespoke goes back to 1906, opened its Haberdashery in 2012. Stocking trousers, knitwear and a full range of accessories (but deliberately *not* ready-made jackets) it was a breath of fresh air for menswear in London.

Today, it feels like part of the furniture in Mayfair. So it's easy to forget how *good* this shop is – how effectively it bridges traditional menswear and modern consumers, and simply what a wonderful experience it is to visit.

The fitting rooms are big, lit by natural light and large black lamps. The furniture is a mix of lovely old wooden fittings and newly commissioned pieces – there can't be many newly commissioned haberdashery cabinets made every year, but Clifford Street has one. The wallpaper, the wood, the mirrors: the feel is sophisticated but comfortable. It's exactly what you would – or should – expect from the ever-tasteful Anda Rowland and Audie Charles.

Trousers were the focus at the beginning, and are still a big part of the offering. The idea is that a customer can have a bespoke jacket made around the corner at the Anderson & Sheppard bespoke atelier on Old Burlington Street, and then come here to pick up two or three pairs of trousers to go with it. There are 12 different models available, ranging from plain, comfortable 'working trousers' to slim-leg ones with side straps or even a Gurkha-style waistband. Around half a dozen colours in each are carried as stock and

PAGE 76 The warm and homely front of the shop.

PAGES 78–79 Anderson & Sheppard is famed for its range of Shetland knitwear.

TOP The Haberdashery provides the perfect accessories to accompany Anderson & Sheppard tailoring.

CENTRE The team at the Haberdashery, from left: Andrzej, Conor, Audie, Emily (left) and Anda (right).

BELOW Haberdashery pieces in autumnal colours (left) and the shop interior (right).

a further half dozen are available for special order from the factory.

The trousers, which are made in Italy, feature nice touches like A&S horn buttons on the waist and the house's signature mother-of-pearl button on the rear pocket. The cloths are largely English, and include very heavy moleskins and drill cottons, as well as brightly coloured linens. A linen drawstring number is particularly popular in summer.

The Haberdashery's second big strength is its knitwear. Most shops do not design the knitwear they stock – as with their ties and handkerchiefs, they essentially relabel the manufacturer's standard designs, picking only which colours, patterns and sizes to carry.

Anda and Audie have done far more than that, changing and redesigning many aspects of the knitwear they offer. Take their shawl-collar cardigan, for example: perhaps the most radical of their redesigns, it is cut short and slim in the body, with a tighter than usual sleeve. The slimness of the body and sleeve means it can fit under a lot

of jackets, while the short body means it sits just on the waistband of regular trousers. It is a world away from the normal, baggy shawl-collar knitwear sold elsewhere. Their Shetland crewneck knitwear is also very popular, and altered to be cut relatively slim in the waist. It comes in a huge variety of colours, from bright orange and pink to more standard browns and greys.

The Haberdashery benefits from knowing its customers very well, and by carrying pieces outside normal fashion seasons – so those Shetlands are still on sale in February when the cold weather in London means they are actually needed. Holiday-weight linens are available year-round.

Other stand-out pieces include the pyjamas and linen dressing gowns, the indigo handkerchiefs and the espadrilles. It's a beautiful range, created by a genuine, impassioned, creative team who have added something unique to the rich variety of London shops.

Melbourne

Australia might not be a country typically associated with fine tailoring and classic menswear, but Melbourne has a good range of shops and makers. This is partly due to the fact that – unlike hotter parts of the country – Melbourne has clear seasons, with a few weeks when something more than a T-shirt is definitely required. It also reflects the culture of the city, which is commonly described as the most European in Australia, with many galleries, shops and (especially) cafés in which to wear more style-conscious clothing.

Melbourne's remote location historically encouraged independent shops in favour of international chains. Although most of the designer brands now have Melbourne branches, it's still easy for home-grown brands to set up and find a local following, especially at a time when the worldwide resurgence of interest in crafted menswear has boosted the city's tailors, shirtmakers and shoemakers.

The List

1 Christian Kimber

christiankimber.com
264 Johnston Street, Fitzroy 3065

See Brand Focus on pages 90–93.

2 Double Monk

www.doublemonk.com
53 Smith Street, Fitzroy 3065

For classic menswear, this is perhaps the finest store in Melbourne (though now with a branch in Sydney). Established by brothers Chris and Nick Schaerf, Double Monk's main focus is on shoes, but it also offers hats, socks, ties and leather accessories. The shoes are mostly from English makers such as Edward Green and Crockett & Jones, along with Alden, Carmina and Saint Crispin's. The shop itself is beautifully outfitted with felt-and-wood shelves and rolling ladders.

3 Pickings & Parry

pickingsandparry.com
3/166 Gertrude Street, Fitzroy 3065

An independent store featuring all types of workwear, Pickings & Parry carries the likes of Nigel Cabourn, Buzz Rickson's and Old Hands. Despite its very different style, this Pickings & Parry shares Double Monk's emphasis on buying only good clothes that last, a philosophy that goes down particularly well with an Australian audience.

4 Masons

www.masonsofficial.com
167 Flinders Lane, Melbourne 3000

Masons is an independent multi-brand store that aims for a luxury audience, but mixes styles including tailoring, high fashion and streetwear. Traditional makers such as Fox Umbrellas and Lock & Co. hatters sit alongside Visvim and Vivienne Westwood, and just across from Jil Sander and Dior Homme. Although led by such brands, there is also a stronger focus on customer service than you will find at most designer stores.

1

5 P. Johnson

pjt.com
1A Crossley Street, Melbourne 3000

P. Johnson, founded in Sydney in 2008 and now with several stores in Australia, as well as branches in London and New York, is the quintessential reflection of Australian style. Its made-to-measure tailoring has always been wonderfully light compared to European pieces, often in pale, earthy colours, and its recent ready-to-wear collections take this a step further with linen shirt-jackets and drawstring trousers in camel or navy. It is worth a visit when more traditional menswear seems a little too heavy for the 40-degree sun.

6 Charles Edwards

8 Crossley St, Melbourne 3000

There aren't many bespoke shirtmakers in Australia, but Charles Edwards in Melbourne has one of the best reputations. Located on Crossley Street, just behind American Tailors and Maimone (both offering bespoke tailoring), Edwards cuts to original paper patterns and is pleasingly non-digital in approach, not even having a basic website.

7 Tolley London W1

www.tolleysavilerow.com
111 Toorak Road, South Yarra 3141

Tolley are perhaps the best of the scattering of old-school bespoke tailors

1

in Melbourne (others include American Tailors, Pino Curcio and Eugenio Nicolini). Certainly they're one of the most modern. Interestingly they own an old Savile Row brand, John Morgan & Co., and offer bespoke suits made in Australia (where they have three in-house tailors) alongside one made by Savile Row coatmakers in a warren-like tailors' den at 11 St George Street in London.

8 Wootten

wootten.com.au
20 Grattan Street, Prahran 3181

9 Roberts & Hassett

roberts-hassett.com.au
**Level 1/2 Somerset Place,
  Melbourne 3000**

These are Melbourne's two finest bespoke shoemakers: Wootten, the old-school name; Roberts & Hassett, the newcomer. Jesse Wootten's shop was founded by his father, who was trained by renowned Bulgarian maker George Koleff. Wootten makes bespoke shoes that are largely machine-sewn in a blake or blake-rapid construction. They can also do hand-stitching but it's only a small part of the business. Roberts & Hassett are young bespoke shoemakers doing only traditional bespoke, with hand-welting, hand-stitched soles and hand-built heels. They are particularly known for using exotic and local leathers, such as kangaroo.

10 Oscar Hunt

www.oscarhunt.com.au
**Level 3, 43 Hardware Lane,
  Melbourne 3000**

11 Calder Sartoria

www.stevecalder.com.au
**Room 305, 37 Swanston Street,
  Melbourne 3000**

Perhaps the two names most worthy of mention for made-to-measure suiting in Melbourne are Oscar Hunt and Steve Calder. Oscar Hunt is a big operator, doing the largest made-to-measure business in Melbourne, with a second location in Sydney. It uses in-store tailors for some of the finishing but the suits are largely made in China. Steve Calder is an ex-Zegna man who offers made-to-measure garments produced in Naples, and stocks brands such as Craftsman Clothiers, Chad Prom and TBD sunglasses.

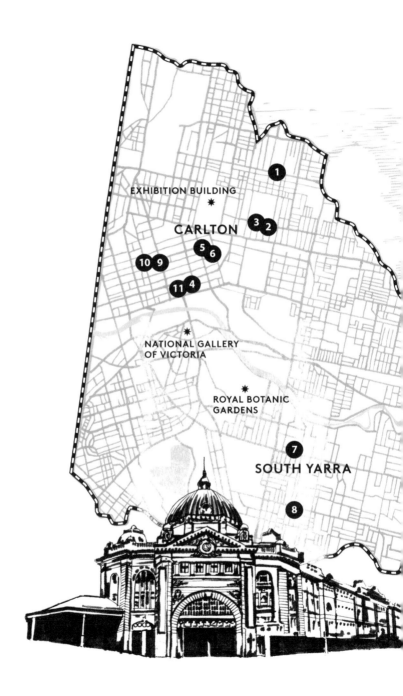

EXHIBITION BUILDING
✳

CARLTON

CARLTON

NATIONAL GALLERY
OF VICTORIA
✳

ROYAL BOTANIC
GARDENS
✳

SOUTH YARRA

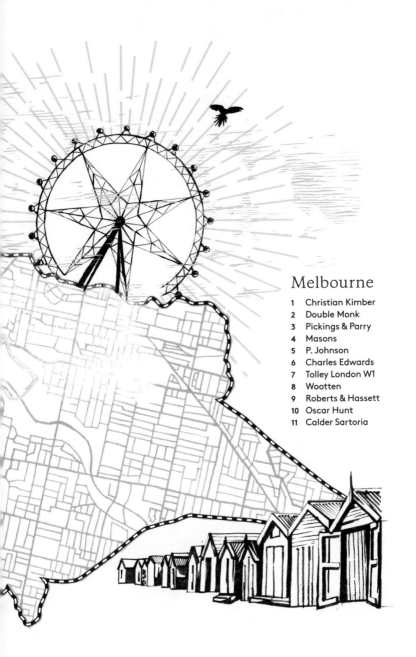

Melbourne

THE EVER CHANGING FACE OF RALPH

Christian Kimber

Helping Australian men to dress in a more sartorial style while remaining faithful to their country's laid-back attitude has become Kimber's mission

Asking men in Australia to dress up is not easy. The heat and famously easy-going culture do not predispose them towards tailoring, leather shoes or even trousers. But Christian Kimber, the British-born founder of his eponymous store in Melbourne's Fitzroy district, is forging a new way.

'For me, what we are offering is the definition of modern, urban Australian style,' he says. 'It's relaxed, it's functional, but it also prioritizes quality materials and ethical production.'

A good example is his Japanese-cotton blousons, which are made from such a soft jersey that they feel like summer knitwear. In navy or a biscuity melange, with cotton lining and a short collar, they are the sort of jacket you could chuck on over anything from jeans to board shorts.

Kimber suggests wearing it with a polo shirt in lightweight Italian piqué, perhaps in dusty pink. An alternative to the blouson is one of his garment-dyed double-breasted jackets made without any canvas or padding – again, more reminiscent of knitwear than of a traditional blazer.

'Most clothing in Australia is either camping, outdoor wear, or formal tailoring that's derived from English style,' says Kimber. 'There's surprisingly little that embraces the new metropolitan, coffee-shop culture of Australian cities.'

Fitzroy is the perfect location to present that new Australian metropolitan style, in an area buzzing with bars, galleries and those ubiquitous coffee shops. The Christian Kimber store is similarly eclectic, with mid-century furniture sitting alongside

LEFT Christian Kimber first became known for his footwear and handkerchiefs.

OPPOSITE ABOVE: A lightweight field jacket.

OPPOSITE BELOW The airy, modernist feel of the shop interior.

PAGE 90 Christian in the shop.

tree-stump coffee tables and stacks of magazines.

'We like the atmosphere to be as comfortable as the clothing,' says Kimber. 'It has a laid-back living-room feel, where guys can just hang out and ask questions without feeling there's a salesman watching their every move.' Many stores pay lip service to this approach, but Kimber is true to his word, offering coffee and other refreshments, and letting the man who

hates shopping slowly get used to how much he likes just being in this shop.

On the walls are framed designs of Kimber's distinctive pocket squares, each of which he drew and designed himself. Inspired by different cityscapes, they feature notably subdued and urban colours, rather different to the yellow polka dots and bright pink paisleys of other men's outfitters. His 'Auckland' square in silk and wool depicts abstract, spiky clouds making landfall on a New Zealand mountain – all in washed blues, greys and browns.

'Australian men often struggle with ideas of masculinity, and in particular where that meets quality clothing,' comments Kimber. 'We show how they can work together, with subtle patterns and colours applied to highly practical pieces.'

Kimber – who founded his brand online four years ago, before opening the physical store in early 2016 – began life as a shoe nerd, working for English shoe brand Lodger before moving to Australia. It's therefore not surprising that his shoe range is both broad and well thought-out, with oxfords and loafers sitting alongside low- and high-top sneakers.

'The footwear is pivotal, in a way,' says Kimber. 'If our jackets and shirts can work equally well with a dressy loafer as a high-top sneaker, then we've done our job.'

Milan

Milan is the centre of the men's fashion industry – yet as far as individual, local style is concerned, interesting shops can be hard to find. Via Montenapoleone, Via della Spiga and the roads that run between are all pleasant places to stroll, but most of the shops that line them belong to large fashion houses with the same offerings that you'll find in any other major city. In this book we try to avoid such cookie-cutter chains. They're certainly not part of the joy of travelling. But look harder in Milan, away from the big flagships, and all sorts of smaller workshops and brands start popping out: big tailors, old shoemakers, and a few independent stores that give the flavour of how Milanese men really shop.

The List

1 Ferdinando Caraceni
caracenisartoria.net
Via San Marco 22, 20121

See Brand Focus on pages 102–05.

2 Stivaleria Savoia
www.stivaleriasavoia.it
Via Francesco Petrarca 7, 20123

See Brand Focus on pages 106–11.

3 Al Bazar
www.albazarmilano.it
Via Antonio Scarpa 9, 20145

This independent menswear shop is top
of the list not for its taste, which isn't
always perfect (e.g. over-coloured double
monks!), but for its originality, in a town
where that can be in short supply. Its
strengths include tailoring in exclusive
cloths, nicely made polo shirts, and some
great knitwear.

4 M. Bardelli
www.mbardelli.com
Corso Magenta 13, 20123

Originally started as a hat business in the
1940s, it is perhaps the best traditional
menswear store in Milan, with a great
range of classic, beautifully made and
luxurious clothing. Bardelli is particularly
good for accessories and knitwear.

5 Tincati
tincatimilano.it
Via Gesù 7, 20121

Although it also has a branch in

New York, Tincati is a quintessentially
Milanese shop with a strong local
following. At home it offers a wider
range that is slightly brighter and bolder
than standard Milanese fare. It is strong
on tailoring, but also has casualwear,
knitwear and accessories.

6 A. Caraceni
caracenimilano.com
Via Fatebenefratelli 16, 20121

7 Musella Dembech
www.muselladembechmilano.com
Via Celestino IV 9, 20123

8 Mario Pecora
www.mariopecora.com
Via Borgospesso 12, 20121

There are, thankfully, still some great
bespoke tailors in Milan, with Ferdinando
Caraceni and Augusto Caraceni on top
of the pile. All are friendly and welcoming
if you drop by unannounced, but it's still
best to make an appointment. If you're
set on bespoke, it's also worth checking
out Musella Dembech and Sartoria
Pecora, among others.

2

9 Rivolta

www.calzoleriarivolta.com
Via della Spiga 17, 20121

At Rivolta shoes are made to very high standards (e.g., hand-sewn welts), with a bespoke service that uses a digital scanner to model the foot. The accuracy of that process has improved substantially in recent years. The shop also offers ready-made shoes in some classic designs and a good range of exotic leathers.

10 Caruso

www.carusomenswear.com
Via Gesù 4, 20121

11 Uman

www.umanconcept.com
Via Gesù 10, 20121

Caruso is a top-class tailoring factory that has expanded in recent years with its own line of ready-to-wear. Although its shops are slowly opening elsewhere around the world, this opera-themed store is worth a visit both for the stock and the interior decoration. Also part of the same company is Uman, around the corner, which is more conservative in colour and pattern but still with innovative cuts and designs. Both are part of the project to turn Via Gesù into a dedicated menswear street.

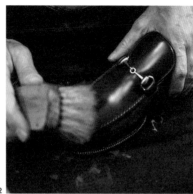

2

12 Maison Siniscalchi

www.siniscalchicamiciesumisura.com
Viale Vittorio Veneto 32, 20124

The best-known of the Milanese shirtmakers, based north of the centre, Siniscalchi offers a nice, if formal make (with floating lining in the collars) and is rather expensive. Other local shirtmakers worth visiting include Evgeniya Kiyan, Camiceria Barone and Alessandra Passeri.

13 Armani

www.armani.com
Via Alessandro Manzoni 31, 20121

If you do want to visit any fashion brands, the massive block of real estate taken up by Giorgio Armani is the one place not to miss in Milan. Whether you love it or hate it, the flagship is an experience, with a café, a flower shop, and menswear from each of the brand's different lines.

DI ANGELI

2

3

4

MUSEO NAZIONALE
DELLA SCIENZA E
DELLA TECNOLOGIA
LEONARDO DA VINCI

7

COLONNE DI
SAN LORENZ

Milan

1 Ferdinando Caraceni
2 Stivaleria Savoia
3 Al Bazar
4 M. Bardelli
5 Tincati
6 A. Caraceni
7 Musella Dembech
8 Mario Pecora
9 Rivolta
10 Caruso
11 Uman
12 Maison Siniscalchi
13 Armani

IBALDI STATION

RTA NUOVA

ERA

GALLERIA VITTORIA
EMMANUELE II

DUOMO

Ferdinando Caraceni

Part of the famous Caraceni dynasty of tailors, this Milanese branch has forged ahead with a passion for craftsmanship passed on from father to daughter

There are several famous tailors with the name Caraceni in Italy. They all stem from Domenico Caraceni and his younger brothers Augusto and Galliano. Two of the Caraceni firms (A. Caraceni and Tommy & Giulio Caraceni) are operated by actual descendants of the founders; another, D. Caraceni, is merely a brand name, run by Gianni Campagna.

The fourth was started by Ferdinando Caraceni, who was not related to Domenico's family despite having the same surname and coming from the same village. He was, however, a cutter at Domenico Caraceni and then at Augusto Caraceni for 29 years.

It is for this reason that the central Italian tailoring style is so homogenous, as so many of the biggest names learnt their style from Domenico.

The operators today are:
- A. Caraceni, run by Carlo and Massimiliano Andreacchio, husband and son of Rita Caraceni (Augusto's granddaughter), in Milan
- Ferdinando Caraceni, run by Nicoletta Caraceni, daughter of Ferdinando Caraceni, in Milan
- Tommy and Giulio Caraceni, sons of Galliano Caraceni, in Rome
- D. Caraceni, brand owned by Gianni Campagna in Milan and focusing on ready-to-wear and made-to-measure

My personal favourite among them is Ferdinando Caraceni. Nicoletta Caraceni has run the firm from the first floor of a town house in the middle of Milan for years, forging ahead with the same level of quality even after her father's death. She has passion, and she has style – the latter

LEFT A Caraceni double-breasted cotton jacket loosely stitched together for a fitting.

OPPOSITE The finished jacket worn by the author at Pitti Uomo in Milan.

PAGE 102 Nicoletta Caraceni at the author's jacket fitting.

something often lacking in the more traditional bespoke tailors. I love the way she still wears her father's blazers, altered and repaired, with other, more feminine, pieces. She brings a lightness to tailoring that most men struggle with.

The Milanese and Roman cutting styles are pretty similar. They are very flattering and remarkably modern, with the softness of much modern tailoring (sitting between the drape styles of London and the ultra-soft ones of Naples), but with a relatively wide, slightly bellied lapel. The modern look is accentuated by a suppressed waist and slightly open foreparts (below the waist button). The style is quite similar to that of Parisian tailors, particularly Cifonelli, which is of course no coincidence: Cifonelli started in Rome, before the founder's son set up the now-dominant Parisian firm.

'The jacket should screw up in the hand, like a handkerchief,' says Nicoletta. 'But it has more shape than the Neapolitans in the collar and the shoulders. It's perfectly possible for a jacket to be so light you forget you're wearing it, yet make you look fantastic.'

Another advantage to visiting the atelier in Milan is the stockpile of vintage cloth available, with a particularly large range of navy pinstripes and chalkstripes on the one end of the spectrum, and pale-coloured cottons and linens on the other.

'Cotton suits and jackets have long been a specialism of ours,' says Nicoletta. 'My father loved them – and he always wanted to make them particularly beautiful, to add more finesse and detailing in order to elevate what is a relatively cheap cloth.'

Some of these old jackets are still on display today, and it's interesting how well they have aged – more like a solid pair of jeans than a lightweight pair of chinos. 'That's the beauty of a heavy cotton,' Nicoletta explains, 'It gains character like nothing else.'

Stivaleria Savoia

A remnant from an age when men wore boots more often than shoes, Stivaleria Savoia is a Milanese institution

Stivaleria Savoia is an old Milanese bespoke bootmaker (*stivaleria* means 'bootmaker'), founded by craftsmen who made footwear for the Savoia (that is, Savoy) cavalry. The original group of craftsmen date back to the 1870s, but the shop itself opened in 1925, initially making boots exclusively.

Today only about 5% of orders are for boots, but they can still make them – the most basic models start at €3600. (They do not make cowboy boots, however, despite some lovely examples being on display.)

The business is largely bespoke, although there is also a ready-made line from Cheaney and made-to-order options manufactured in Milan. The styles are classic, practical and very good value, with bespoke shoes starting at €2000.

The bespoke designs are all fairly traditional and understated, with a range of round and square toe shapes, and relatively square waists and heels. Monk straps are particularly prominent. Savoia does offer a narrower, more bevelled waist, but most orders are for the squarer, flatter styles.

Famous customers over the years have included Italian, Moroccan and French royalty, as well as film stars new and old, among them Sylvester Stallone.

As is often the case with storied craftsmen, the shop operates a beautiful book-based order system that involves one index volume and then several others containing measurements and order details.

Savoia has five craftsmen: managing director Fausto Risi, who does all the measuring and last-

ABOVE LEFT The bespoke workshop at Savoia.

THESE PAGES Sample shoes on display in the shop, including the boots that were its original focus.

OVERLEAF A bespoke loafer being made (left) and a finished four-buckle boot (right).

PAGE 106 Fausto and Silvia Risi outside the shop.

making; his wife Silvia, who does all the cutting; and head shoemaker Filippo Ballatore, who works with two other makers.

A lovely aspect of Savoia is that the workshop is right in the shop, with all the dust, grime and tools that prove you're getting a handmade and highly sweated product. The workshop is behind glass, so none of that dust can contaminate the wood-panelled shop, but customers are encouraged to step inside and see the work in progress.

I love visible on-site workshops like this one (and at John Lobb in London). Value is hard enough to communicate at the best of times. If it is physical and as difficult to ignore as a man stitching a welt, it should be put front and centre.

Even if classic, practical shoes are not what you're looking for, pop into Savoia to experience its history and craftsmanship, as well as for the range of ties and other accessories.

Naples

Naples has the highest concentration of high-end handmade menswear in the world. For tailoring and shirtmaking (though less so for shoes) this is the motherlode, with hundreds of tailors in the city and surrounding region, and thousands working in small factories or busily hand-sewing at home. Most menswear enthusiasts will visit Naples at some point, for a fitting or just to see the atelier of the tailor they've been using for years – and to give some context to those beautiful suits they wear every day. You come here for bespoke, not for shopping. But there are still a few shops worth visiting, which I've presented alongside groupings of some of the best tailors and shirtmakers. Naples is home to so many excellent bespoke artisans that it is impossible to name them all individually, so the bespoke listings in this chapter can only be partial and subjective.

The List

1 Mario Talarico

www.mariotalarico.it
Vico Due Porte a Toledo 4/B, 80134

See Brand Focus on pages 120–23.

2 Barbarulo

www.gemellidapolso.it/en
**Piazza Amedeo 16/I,
  Passeggiata Colonna, 80121**

See Brand Focus on pages 124–27.

3 Cerrato

www.instagram.com/cerratomarco/
Via Emanuele de Deo 4, 80134

See Brand Focus on pages 128–31.

4 Rubinacci

www.marianorubinacci.net
Via Chiaia 149/E, 80121

Historically the biggest tailoring house
in Naples and the place so many other
greats have sprung from, Rubinacci
moved a few years ago from its old,
curved-front shop into a much larger
space up on the hill. Here it looks down

impressively on the Via Chiaia, although
its elevated position can also make it easy
to miss. The new premises have a large,
deep shop selling both Rubinacci ready-
to-wear and a variety of accessories, and
a bespoke space at the back with many
bolts on display. If possible, try to see the
cloth archive, which is stored in an actual
bank vault.

5 E. Marinella

www.marinellanapoli.it
Riviera di Chiaia 287, 80122

Perhaps the most famous shop in Naples,
the original Marinella premises is
shockingly small. There is just about
enough room for two people to come in,
browse the famous ties that are stacked
unceremoniously in plastic sleeves on
the tables, buy one and leave. Various
Marinella spin-offs are also available
around the shop, and upstairs, but it
is the ties and the charm of the tiny
boutique that people come for.

6 E. & G. Cappelli

www.patriziocappelli.it
Via Cavallerizza 37, 80121

The other internationally known Neapolitan
tiemaker is bigger, but harder to find.
Cappelli's shop (and workshop) is located
in the gated square at 37 Via Cavallerizza.
You'll have to ring to get through the gate;
once inside, you can also visit Sartoria
Formosa – for tailoring or shirts – on other
sides of the square. Another tie brand that
has opened a shop in Naples, and is worth
a visit given how close and central it is, is
Ulturale on Via Carlo Poerio.

2

7 Caccioppoli

www.caccioppolinapoli.it
Via Antonio Ciccone 8, 80133

There used to be dozens of cloth merchants in Naples, importing and stocking cloth from Biella and Huddersfield for all the tailors around the city. Today there is only one: Caccioppoli. The Caccioppoli offices, on three floors covering most of a city block in the east end of Naples, have a lovely atmosphere. Customers can buy cloth directly from the shop, which is unusual among cloth merchants, and visitors to Naples should take advantage of the chance to see the latest season's collections in full bolts.

8 Camiceria Piccolo

www.camiceriapiccolo.com
Via Chiaia 41, 80132

Far, far smaller than Caccioppoli, but still worth a visit, Camiceria Piccolo (not to be confused with shirtmaker Salvatore Piccolo) is a small shirtings shop just off Via Chiaia in the centre of town. The range of shirtings is good, if not extraordinary. There are few rare or unusual bolts you won't find elsewhere (in contrast to, say, the Charvet range in Paris), but actual shops with this volume of shirtings on display are few and far between. Take the opportunity to consider shirt fabrics, their textures and weaves more closely.

9 Milord

Via Cavallerizza 53, 80121

Visitors to Naples with an interest in classic menswear will welcome the number of small shops offering brands such as Incotex, Boglioli and other Italian smart/casual labels. There are no more such shops here in Naples than you'll find in Rome and Milan,

but far more than there are in the UK, US or Asia. Milord on Via Cavallerizza is a good example of such a shop. Most are relatively cheap and perhaps even a little outdated, but it's always interesting to pop in on the lookout for a nice tie or chino.

10 Sartoria Rifugio

www.alfredorifugio.com
Via Bonifica 30, trav. Vicinale di Palma, 84018 Pompeii (NA)

11 Sartoria Melina

www.melinaemme.it
www.instagram.com/
sartoriamelinanapoli/
Via Provinciale Amendola 39/O, trav. Monturiello, 84087 Sarno (SA)

As you might expect among the hundreds of tailors in Naples, there are a few who specialize in leather work: for brands, for tailors, making garments under their own name, or all three. The biggest and best-known is Sartoria Rifugio, which also has showrooms in Milan, New York and Palm Beach, though Naples is its hometown. Sartoria Melina, which only does bespoke, fully handmade work, is a smaller company, founded in 2016 by one of the top makers at Rifugio, Carmela Caruso, who branched out on her own. Both produce a lightweight leather or suede jacket – no canvas, just a small shoulder pad and a thin layer of fusing. The handwork is beautiful, and the nubuck calfskin is a particularly nice choice. Both are some way out of town – Rifugio in Pompeii and Melina in nearby Sarno – and require appointments.

12 Sartoria Panico

sartoriapanico.it
Via Giosuè Carducci 29, 80121

13 Sartoria Solito

sartoriasolito.it
Via Toledo 256, 80132

14 Sartoria Dalcuore

sartoriadalcuore.com
Via Francesco Caracciolo 17, 80122

15 Sartoria Ciardi

www.sartoriaciardi.com
Via Giuseppe Fiorelli 12, 80121

16 Sartoria Caliendo

sartoriacaliendo.com
Via Santa Maria di Cappella
  Vecchia 6, 80121

Some of the great names of Neapolitan tailoring – such as Antonio Panico, Antonio Pascariello, Gennaro Solito and Gigi Dalcuore – are still around and working, and worth a visit. It's much easier to arrange one if you are having something made, and commissioning a suit in Naples remains very good value for money (although it will require several return trips for fittings unless your tailor also travels). Their ateliers are steeped in history, with various awards and certificates on the walls. The premises of Panico and Ciardi are also decorated with tailoring accessories, such as old irons, and paintings that make the place feel more like a home than a shop. Which of course, is exactly how they want it. Smaller or younger tailors are more likely to travel, and among them it's worth seeking out Elia Caliendo in the centre of town. Dalcuore also travels widely.

17 Ambrosi

Ambrosi-napoli.tumblr.com
Via Chiaia 184, 80132

There are two young and dynamic men at the head of two of the trouser-makers in Naples: Marco Cerrato (see pages 128–31) and Salvatore Ambrosi. Both are very welcoming and make great trousers. Ambrosi has already become well-known around the world, both for bespoke and ready-to-wear. Like Cerrato, Ambrosi generally offers a higher level of make (more bar tacks, more pick stitching) under his own name than in the trousers he also produces for the city's tailors.

18 Luca Avitabile

www.lucavitabile.it
Via Toledo 256, 80132

19 Anna Matuozzo

anna-matuozzo.tumblr.com
Viale Antonio Gramsci 26, 80122

20 D'Avino

davinoshirt.tumblr.com
Via Marigliano 72, 80049 Somma
  Vesuviana (NA)

There are a lot of shirtmakers in Naples, most of whom are open to visitors but tend not to have ateliers with the same history and atmosphere as the great tailors. Luca Avitabile has built an international business for his bespoke and ready-made polo shirts (designed with Permanent Style). In 2017 he also opened a large office on Via Toledo (in the same building as Sartoria Solito), which is modern and welcoming, with a lovely view down the long shopping street. Anna Matuozzo is one of the most famous makers and uses more handwork in her shirts. Outside of town, meanwhile, is D'Avino bespoke (not to be confused with Avino, which does both ready-made and bespoke). If you fancy travelling out to the suburbs, the D'Avino atelier is in a pleasant suburb and is surrounded by the factories of bigger Neapolitan brands like Attolini and Borrelli, as well as many women finishing shirts at home.

Naples

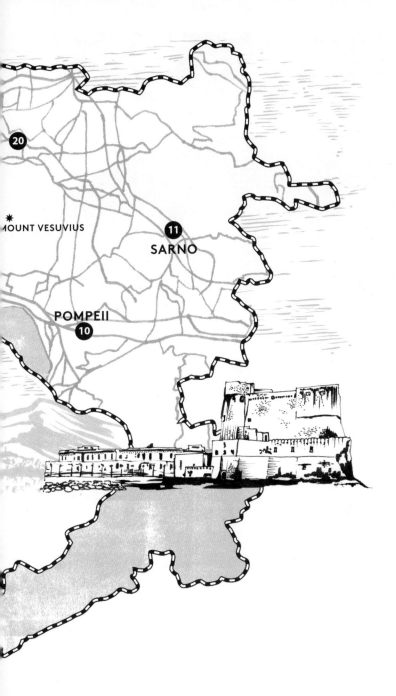

Talarico

An unlikely master, Mario Talarico can be found tucked inside a brightly glowing shop in the Spanish quarter of Naples

The atelier of Mario Talarico is one of the least prepossessing of any master craftsman. Sitting in a tiny alley off the Via Toledo in Naples, it is festooned with cheap, tacky umbrellas. Most cost €10; all are made in China.

There is clearly demand for them, despite the Mediterranean weather, because Mario actually has two shops, one on each side of the alley. Both are equally unattractive.

It is only by picking the correct shop, on the left as you ascend the hill, and letting your eyes adjust to the darkness when you enter, that you discern that this is the workshop of a very fine umbrella maker.

The drawers were the first thing I noticed. Two rows of them, in ancient wood, as you find in old apothecary tables. Yellowed labels indicated that they contained a variety of small metal parts. There was certainly craft going on here.

Next, below them, the workbench, which Mario says is almost 200 years old. Given that the company was founded in 1860, that means it was pretty well used before Mario's predecessors acquired it; now, it is dilapidated. A whole chunk of the front has been worn away, as if a shark has taken a huge bite out of it. It is covered in sawdust from the drilling machine that is used to bore holes in the umbrella handles and tips. A small stool sits between the two, under a low shelf so that Mario – who is not small – has to crouch slightly as he works.

Before we get too Dickensian, it should be said that Mario's nephew, Mario Jr, works standing behind the counter, where he has all the room and light he requires. Indeed, the light is reflected and multiplied by the scores of framed pictures that hang around him: Mario with the Pope, Mario with Fendi, Mario with Berlusconi. A dozen more cuttings are preserved under the glass counter-top. Some are suspended from the ceiling.

And then, last of all, you notice the umbrellas. They are camouflaged (like herds of long-necked gazelles) by their sheer numbers, stacked close and several deep behind

the counter and hanging on the opposite wall.

Many are in plastic sheaths. But the handles absorb your attention, once you notice them: beech, chestnut, cherrywood, Malacca and bamboo, all carefully and patiently worked with steam into a curve of (at least) 180 degrees. Each piece of wood is carefully selected so that a bulbous, polished knob remains on the end of the handle, like a crown. The rest is

ABOVE The shop in the crowded Spanish Quarter.

LEFT A finished umbrella in patterned green silk.

BELOW Mario Talarico with his workbench and tools.

ABOVE AND LEFT Mario Talarico Jr sews a piece of silk over the opening mechanism (left) and then tests the finished umbrella (above).

FAR LEFT The shop interior.

PAGE 120 A finished umbrella opened outside the shop.

clipped and polished, but not whittled, down its length until it finishes, on the other side of the canopy, with a chunk of pale buffalo horn.

There is something very satisfying in the making of an immediately practical, useful object like an umbrella. With speed bordering on showing off, Mario cuts a slit in the shaft and inserts a metal hairpin; he then aligns the metal cylinder that holds all the metal arms of the canopy and brings the two together several times, tweaking the pin with a pair of pliers until the connection is perfect and the umbrella simply snaps shut.

Mario Jr sews on the canopy by hand, with little strips of the same waterproof cloth from which it is made, and then creates the skirt that will protect the central mechanism from rust. He slices off each piece of cloth, by eye, with a big pair of shears. All nice touches that are impossible to achieve by machine.

Mario is dismissive of other umbrella-makers. It is the justifiable pride of a man who has been making umbrellas all his life and has been asked scores of times to expand, to produce for other brands and retailers. His nephew is more generous. Both are fervently committed to making umbrellas by hand for years to come. This only seems incongruous when you leave the workshop and once again see, on a child's plastic umbrella hanging from the other shop, Mickey Mouse staring inanely across the Due Porte.

Barbarulo

**An old jewellery name has been reinvigorated with a
new focus on craft in the store – and on new men's ranges
for an age when few wear cufflinks every day**

Jewellery has been in the Barbarulo family for four generations. The company was founded in 1894 by a goldsmith, Raffaele Barbarulo; his son Amedeo was a trader in precious stones; current owner Cristiano's father, also called Raffaele, moved the shop to Capri and sold vintage jewellery. And in 2012, Cristiano opened the family's current shop in a lovely arcade next to Piazza Amedeo in Naples to focus again on jewellery manufacturing.

Barbarulo in its modern incarnation is closely associated with menswear. It is best known for cufflinks, and its Italian site is actually called Gemellidapolso.it (Italian for 'cufflinks'). In that guise it has made links for many famous people and films, including Michael Caine in the film *Youth* (2015), Geoffrey Rush in *The Best Offer* (2013) and to accompany the Attolini tailoring in Paolo Sorrentino's *La Grande Bellezza* (The Great Beauty) (2013).

In recent years, Cristiano has also been trying to move production back into the shop itself, which was what got us interested. Today about half of the production is done in Caserta, outside Naples, in a lab owned by Barbarulo. The other half is done in the shop, where the precious metals are cut down, polished and inlaid with stones. Enamelwork and stone-cutting are done offsite, in the Caserta workshop.

Interestingly, very few men wear cufflinks in Naples. More do in the north of Italy, although still fewer than in England. In Italy cufflinks are considered a very particular gift – something precious that it's possible

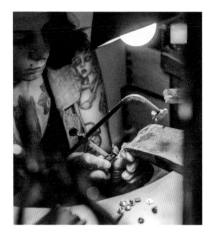

cabochon stones or silver figures attached to gold, silver or stone-bead chains with sections of coral or similar decorations on the other end.

Elsewhere, Cristiano has plenty of 'fun' cufflinks – propellers, winches and aphorisms – which will always be popular with a certain type of customer. But the majority of his pieces are quite simple and refined, featuring amber, lapis lazuli, onyx or mother-of-pearl, inlaid in silver or gold. 'The real Neapolitan style in jewellery is for small, subtle pieces,' says Cristiano. 'Nothing showy, not really. This is what we have always done and what we try to produce today.' The design Barbarulo is best known for is a simple coral design, mounted on gold with a single diamond.

Cristiano keeps a selection of his father's antique pieces on display in the shop for inspiration, along with the marriage certificate of his great-grandfather, Raffaele, the founder. And on four walls of the front room are four shots of the family's previous shops: the 1920, 1940, 1950 and 1980 incarnations of the company. Cristiano's personal collection includes a lot of vintage buttons, which he collects on trips around Italy and elsewhere, and occasionally turns into cufflink designs.

If you're ever in Naples, the store – in a little sunken arcade just off Piazza Amedeo – is worth a visit to see the antiques and the company's full range of pieces, and to watch some of the metal- and gem-work being done on location.

to give a man, and probably only rarely worn. Cristiano would like to encourage people to wear them every day, which is the reason he gives for having designs or stones on only one side of the cuff to make his cufflinks easier to put on.

Barbarulo makes other men's accessories, including lapel chains and money clips. Cristiano recently introduced a range of lapel chains that clients can customize, picking the stone, chain and pendant individually. Options include gold buttons,

RIGHT Vintage pins.

BELOW Vintage buttons.

BOTTOM RIGHT A piece of coral to adorn a cufflink.

BOTTOM LEFT A classic Barbarulo cufflink design.

PAGE 124 Cristiano Barbarulo.

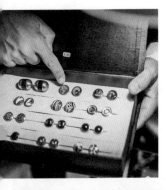

Cerrato

**One of the most atmospheric ateliers in Naples
is that of trouser-maker Cerrato, on the first floor
of a building in the Spanish Quarter of town**

The Spanish Quarter, though central, is one of the city's oldest and poorest areas. It is here that you are most likely to hear the Neapolitan dialect, and its streets – running up the hill from Via Toledo – are still best avoided late at night. The Cerrato family house is halfway up one of these streets. The atelier is two streets over. And Marco Cerrato, who runs the atelier today, lives three streets beyond that. This is still a community, in the middle of the modern city.

The door to the building that houses the atelier is huge and wooden, designed originally to admit a cart and horses. A small cutaway in it allows pedestrians to step through. The inner courtyard is dark and, frankly, very dirty. But it breathes history, and the broad stone steps up to the first floor are cool and shadowy. The atelier itself comprises two rooms: a workshop

and an office/cutting room. In the workshop are Marco's mother, his father, his wife and one of his brothers (the other, Massimo, lives in London and does fittings there).

Historically, there have been a handful of trouser workshops like this in Naples (the other big ones are Mola and Ambrosi) working nearly exclusively for tailors. The tailors would take measurements and sometimes cut the patterns, before handing on the work to the trouser workshop. But in recent years the trouser-makers have begun to establish their own brands, and serve their own customers direct. Ambrosi was the trailblazer in this, but Cerrato also began to do so a few years ago and now nearly half of its business is retail.

'It's important to maintain a balance, but I do like working directly with customers,' says Marco. 'It's

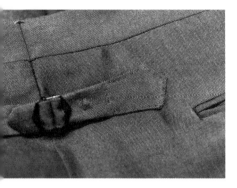

ABOVE A hand-sewn trouser strap.

RIGHT Founder Ciro Cerrato, Marco's father.

BELOW Marco Cerrato and his wife.

PAGE 128 Marco on the street outside the shop.

more personal and more satisfying. Those customers also appreciate a higher level of handwork, or have more interesting design ideas.'

He estimates that work for tailors (four, currently) can produce about 115 pairs a week. But the extra work often required for end customers means that number is more like 80 a week.

Those trousers aren't all made by the family in the workshop. An additional 17 people work from home. They tend to do the finishing work, such as the pick stitching, bar tacks and buttonholes. This arrangement used to be common in many parts of Europe, and there are still remnants of it in the UK or France (for hand-rolled handkerchief hems, for example). But in Naples, where the lack of industrialization left many traditional handcrafts intact, homeworking remains especially common.

Quality in trouser-making tends to come down to how thoroughly and precisely the sewing is done: do buttons fall off; is the stitching so loose that lining starts to come away? Or, for instance, if a trouser-maker is asked to do a waistband that is wider than standard, will he use the same narrow lining, or cut an entirely new one from a full roll of canvas (as Marco does).

When it comes to cutting, there are some small differences in style – or 'handwriting', as Marco puts it. 'I tend to prefer a little more room around the top, the seat,' he says. 'I hate it when the cloth pulls there. And then I would narrow the leg slightly more sharply below the knee.'

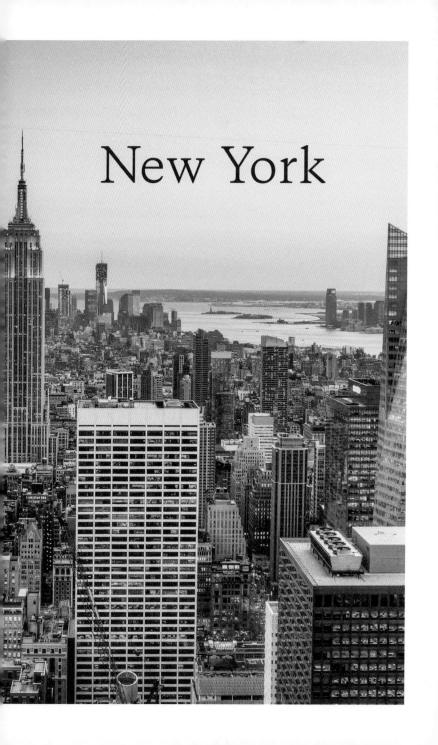

New York

New York is a strange town for menswear. It's a bit of a Wild West, without the established sartorial traditions you find in Europe – one reason why so much bespoke tailoring is provided by visitors from Savile Row. If there is a New York tradition, it is for value: low-priced sack suits that are constantly on offer. So where does the crafted, sartorial menswear fit in? Around the edges, largely: in imports like The Armoury, online warehouses like No Man Walks Alone, and the odd diamond-in-the-rough such as Leffot. One advantage New York has, however, is that the relatively conservative tastes of its male shoppers have kept department stores such as Bergdorf Goodman and Paul Stuart focused on traditional menswear – in contrast with London, where there is increasingly too much fashion (Selfridges) or bling (Harrods). So we have many reasons to thank these well-off American men who value European tradition – not least because were it not for them, most Savile Row tailors would have gone out of business years ago.

The List

1 No Man Walks Alone

www.nomanwalksalone.com
336 W. 37th Street, 10018

See Brand Focus on pages 140–43.

2 Leffot

leffot.com
10 Christopher Street, 10014

See Brand Focus on pages 144–49.

3 Paul Stuart

www.paulstuart.com
354 Madison Avenue, 10017

See Brand Focus on pages 150–53.

4 The Armoury

thearmoury.com
168 Duane Street, 10013

The New York branch of the shop founded in Hong Kong (see pages 54–59) has not only brought great brands like Ring Jacket, Saint Crispin's and Carmina to New York, but also hosts a regular series of bespoke artisans. The offering is slightly different to that of the Hong Kong shop – for example, the ready-to-wear trousers offered by Neapolitan maker Pommella, who also visits only the New York store for trunk shows.

5 Bergdorf Goodman

www.bergdorfgoodman.com
754 5th Avenue, 10019

As mentioned, Bergdorf's has managed to remain one of the most traditional (luxury) department stores in recent years. It still has category sections for much of the clothing on display, rather than just shop-in-shops, and the staff are knowledgeable.

6 Len Logsdail

leonardlogsdail.com
9 E. 53rd Street, 10022

Bespoke tailors have a hard time in New York, because Savile Row has been coming here for such a long time and has a committed client base. Len Logsdail is one Englishman who stayed, and he cuts a very fine suit. Also worthy of mention are Joseph Genuardi, Frank Shattuck, and the soft tailoring of Mark Rykken, who used to be at Paul Stuart and now runs his own shop called Britches Bespoke. Oh, and of course Alan Flusser – if you grew up with *Dressing the Man*, always worth a visit.

2

7 Miller's Oath
www.millersoath.com
510 Greenwich Street, 10013

Listed here for its style as well as its neat made-to-measure tailoring. Founder Kirk Miller manages to consistently bring a contemporary view to classic men's style, and he stocks some nice accessories.

8 Vincent & Edgar shoes
972 Lexington Avenue, 10021

One of very few bespoke shoemakers in New York. Craftsman Ramon makes shoes for Gay Talese, among others.

9 Freeman's Sporting Club
freemanssportingclub.com
8 Rivington Street, 10002

Most of the tailoring at Freeman's Sporting Club is a little narrow and short – call it 'contemporary'. But the atmosphere of the shop and the styling are wonderful, as are the little gems often displayed around the walls. Worth a visit.

10 Worth & Worth hats
www.hatshop.com
50 E. 57th Street, 10022

Showcasing designs by Orlando Palacios, this is probably the best hat shop in New York. A key strength is its blending of classic styles with modern colours and shapes. Most hat shops are either very traditional or very young and funky, but Palacios's designs manage to reach across the divide.

11 Self Edge
www.selfedge.com
157 Orchard Street, 10002

12 Blue in Green
blueingreensoho.com
8 Greene Street, 10013

13 Levi's
www.levi.com
414 W. 14th Street, 10014

As you would expect, New York has a great range of denim shops. The Levi's store in the Meatpacking District is worth listing for its bespoke jeans, which come highly recommended. Self Edge and Blue in Green have a good range of Japanese brands – and their own chain-stitch machines.

14 Geneva
genevacustomshirts.com
65 W. 55th Street #2a, 10019

15 CEGO
www.cego.com
254 5th Avenue, 3rd Floor, 10001

As with tailors and cordwainers, New York doesn't have a large number of bespoke shirtmakers, but if you want someone local then both Geneva and CEGO custom shirts are worth a try. Geneva also does alterations on shirts and trousers, while CEGO offers both a made-to-measure and a bespoke ('full custom') service.

THE MET ✳

CENTRAL PARK
✳

⑧

⑤
⑭ ⑩
TIMES SQUARE
✳
⑥

① ③

EMPIRE STATE
BUILDING ✳
GRAND CENTRAL
STATION ✳

⑮

⑬ MANHATTAN

②

⑦

⑫ ⑨ ⑪

④

BROOKLYN BRIDGE ✳

138

New York

No Man Walks Alone

The online store you should travel to see, No Man Walks Alone has developed a cult following in New York for its sophisticated selection of both formal and casual clothing

No Man Walks Alone (NMWA) is primarily an online shop, and arguably shouldn't be in this guide. But it is a great example of a new type of independent store: one that begins online, as the easiest and quickest way to set up, and then evolves over time into something more akin to a showroom, with consultations by appointment, visiting artisans and a focus on customer service.

Founded by ex-banker Greg Lellouche, the site takes its name from a line Humphrey Bogart says to Audrey Hepburn in *Sabrina*. The name evokes a community of like-minded men – and in the case of NMWA, one centred around well-considered, craft-based clothing. Greg started NMWA at a time when there were few places to see curated menswear online. Sites like Mr Porter were in their infancy,

and there was little else that he could browse from his desk on Wall Street as a distraction from the daily grind of high finance. Greg had visited bespoke tailors, and was an enthusiast for both English and Italian tailoring, but he also wanted to find casual brands with a similar emphasis on craft and quality.

NMWA's online store offers a broad range of tailoring options, including Sartoria Formosa and Eidos for suits and jackets, and Italian factory Rota for trousers. It also features streetwear brands like Robert Geller, Norwegian Rain and James Grose – all of which are particularly strong on outerwear, with James Grose offering leather and suede jackets, Norwegian Rain interesting weather-proofs, and Robert Geller a fresh and idiosyncratic range of coats and jackets each season.

LEFT A Sartoria Formosa suit ready for a customer.

such as Florentine/Japanese tiemaker Tie Your Tie, American bag-maker Frank Clegg, Hungarian shoemaker Vass and Irish knitter Inis Meáin – quite an international bunch. Greg and his team consider these special orders and events to be an integral part of the customer service they provide.

Personalized customer service is central to NMWA's identity. By email, phone and social media, the NMWA team spend hours answering questions, providing extra measurements and giving advice on how a specific jacket will fit with a clothing collection. 'Some guys have been customers for so long now that we know their wardrobes inside out,' says Greg. 'We can advise them on what from the new collections will round out what they already have, or perhaps give some variation to their tailoring rotation. It's all about that interaction – and people take advantage of it whether they're in Colorado or Manhattan.'

That kind of personal service is something physical stores aspire to, but rarely fulfil. Salesmen come and go; the owner rarely has time to be on the shop floor. An online store has more flexibility to do that, and NMWA has been able to bring that experience into a physical space in their showroom as well. It's worth making an appointment to experience the service in person.

The physical office-cum-showroom is on an upper floor of a block in New York's Garment District. It is popular with regular customers who frequently come in to try on new pieces. Although the NMWA team photographs stock themselves (to make comparisons between brands easier) and provides as much fitting information as possible, they appreciate that nothing quite compares to seeing the products in person. Artisans such as Sartoria Formosa also hold regular trunk shows at the showroom, offering bespoke and made-to-measure tailoring.

In recent years Greg and the team have started doing pop-ups in Midtown Manhattan, inviting customers down to the showroom to see the new stock for the season, try on everything and get in on special orders. Special orders involve brands

THIS PAGE Shoes, shirts and tailoring at a No Man Walks Alone event.

PAGE 140 Founder Greg Lellouche.

Leffot

A trailblazer for independent, high-end
retail in men's shoes, Leffot has become
a mecca for men in New York

When Leffot was founded in New York in 2008, it was unusual: a specialist high-end men's shoe store in a city dominated by big department stores. But Steven Taffel knew what he was doing. He prioritized customer service and deep knowledge of the products, and within a few years had developed a strong client base and an international reputation.

Leffot now has branches in New York and Chicago, and has helped to inspire a trend of other specialist men's shoe stores around the world. These stores tend to concentrate on smaller shoe brands that put a lot of handwork into their product: Edward Green from Northampton, the traditional home of English shoemaking; and Saint Crispin's from Romania, one of very few brands still offering ready-made shoes with a hand-sewn welt.

Walk into Leffot today and the atmosphere is friendly, open and refined. The focus is unequivocally on the product: a long bench dominates the space, stretching most of the length of the store, with the shoes displayed proudly down its length. You are invited to circulate and examine the workmanship: the patination on a Corthay oxford, or the depth of colour on an Alden cordovan boot.

'The challenge, certainly when we started, was getting New York guys to pay attention to the product,' says Steven. 'Even downtown in the Village, where we are, everyone is in a rush, and they'd just pop in because they saw something bright and shapely in the window. The price tag would often make them raise their eyebrows. Then it was a case of explaining why the shoe was worth that much.'

A decade later, Steven has built up a solid and loyal clientele who know all about the shoes. They'll pop in asking about a new model that's expected any day, or refer to a particular shape of shoe by the maker's numerical code – 'the 202 last', for example. But there is still that walk-by traffic, the guys who like a sharp shoe and are attracted by the unusual Enzo Bonafé button boot. They come in, get chatting, and before they know it are deep into learning about shoemaking traditions and the finer arts of boar-bristle stitching.

'Once you start talking about the shoe, it's relatively easy to tell whether someone is interested or not, and therefore whether it's worth pursuing,' says Steven. 'Some guys really love shoes, obsess about them; many do not, but there are quite a few who find it fascinating, and see the value quickly.'

Leffot's range has evolved since the shop first opened, with fewer niche specialist brands such as Aubercy and Artioli, and a few more American-made shoes such as Alden. This has partly been for reasons of diversity (the latter is typically under $800, whereas most of the higher-end brands are over $1200) and partly a reaction to the increased interest in American products among customers.

Leffot also offers a great range of Pantherella socks, Saphir shoecare products, buffalo-horn accessories and menswear add-ons such as gloves and cordovan watch straps. It has become particularly known for the latter, and other cordovan products such as 'The Fold', a simple T-shaped piece of horse leather that folds up to become a sleek billfold.

If this book is to be any kind of guide to the world's finest menswear stores, it needs to highlight not just the product – which, of course, can be bought elsewhere – but the place and the people. It is with this in mind that I recommend visiting Leffot in New York (or Chicago) and starting a conversation. If you visit at the end of the day, you may even be offered a glass of whisky from the back. And then the talk really gets going.

Paul Stuart

Paul Stuart is how menswear stores used to be – and, in many people's eyes, how they always should be

The Paul Stuart store on Madison Avenue is big. Its various sections cater to every part of a man's wardrobe: accessories in the front; casualwear in the back; and whole galleries of formalwear upstairs. Each department feels comprehensive: the selection of knitted ties is a rainbow, with every colour you can imagine; the socks cover every shade of trouser a man could ever want to match.

In an age dominated by fashion, it's good to know that most things at Paul Stuart don't change from season to season. There will always be new things, new ideas; but here you can always find that navy overcoat or brown leather jacket.

Most department stores used to be like this. They were divided into departments, each covering one aspect of a man's requirements. Then the stores all slowly turned into malls, merely offering smaller versions of the designer shops available elsewhere.

Paul Stuart has the spirit of just such an old, high-end store. When you ask a member of staff for help or advice, they will display not only extensive knowledge of the product, but genuine taste in how it could be worn. I once observed an old (and very well-dressed) New Yorker come into Paul Stuart and show an assistant a leather jacket he'd bought 30 years ago in the store. The leather was ageing well, but the chain in the collar for hanging it had come loose. Within five minutes the assistant had located a new chain and a pair of pliers, and had replaced the broken piece. Try getting someone in Selfridges to do that.

In recent years Paul Stuart has undergone a mild overhaul in style,

spearheaded by the introduction of the Phineas Cole line, which introduced younger, bolder styles and sharper cuts that later fed through to the main collection. If the store ever had a failing, it was not keeping up to speed with what a younger (but still very well-dressed) man might want, so this change was welcome. Alongside the classic navy and grey suits, it is now possible to find double-monk shoes, reversible gilets, and coats in exploded Prince of Wales check. The latter, as with the suiting, will likely come with a waistcoat and peak lapels if it is part of the Phineas Cole line. Paul Stuart now has stores in Chicago and Washington DC, but the original store in New York is the most impressive and most worth going out of your way to visit.

ABOVE LEFT The range of Paul Stuart footwear, most of which is Goodyear-welted in the UK.

ABOVE RIGHT AND OPPOSITE Summery tailoring with colourful accessories.

PAGE 150 The interior of the recently redecorated store.

Paris

Paris, unlike London or Milan, has never been internationally famous as a centre of menswear (women's couture is another story) – yet it is home to a surprisingly broad range of small companies and artisans. The products are often high-end, as the city's couture heritage has long nurtured a tradition of fine but expensive tailoring and shoemaking, supported by a rich stream of international visitors. Although Paris has few independent, multi-brand boutiques, it boasts an enormous number of artisans who are at the top of their game and unique to the city.

The List

1 Heurtault
www.parasolerieheurtault.com
Viaduc des Arts, 85 Avenue Daumesnil, 75012

See Brand Focus on pages 162–67.

2 Charvet
www.charvet.com
28 Place Vendôme, 75001

See Brand Focus on pages 168–71.

3 Corthay
www.corthay.com
1 Rue Volney, 75002

See Brand Focus on pages 172–77.

4 Cifonelli
www.cifonelli.com
31 Rue Marbeuf, 75008

5 Camps de Luca
campsdeluca.com
16 Rue de la Paix, 75002

Paris has a small but very good bespoke tailoring scene. French bespoke suits are generally characterized by soft structure but strong shoulder lines, with the best finishing in the world. The three best-known houses are Cifonelli (now clearly the biggest), Camps de Luca and Smalto (which also has a rather gaudy ready-to-wear line). The first two are recommended most highly.

6 Cifonelli ready-to-wear
www.cifonelli.com
83 Rue du Faubourg Saint-Honoré, 75008

Cifonelli has also expanded into ready-to-wear in recent years, with its first store on Rue du Faubourg Saint-Honoré. It operates separately from the bespoke business, and though there are some elements (such as its distinctive roped shoulder) that bespoke customers will recognize, the aesthetic is quite different: cream, black, velvet and many things for a dramatic evening look, along with some beautiful silk/cashmere knitwear. Currently it is the brand's only standalone store in the world, although another is planned in London.

4

7 Berluti bespoke

www.berluti.com
9 Rue du Faubourg Saint-Honoré, 75008

The Berluti empire is by no means unique
to Paris. But this is where the brand was
founded, and where its bespoke tailoring
is located, following a takeover of the
old Arnys workshop. It is also the base
of Berluti's bespoke shoemaking, which
has been expanded with a few finely
chosen artisans. If either appeals, then
Paris is the place to go for consultations
and fittings. (And try to forget the sad
demise of Arnys, which would be on this
list if it still existed.)

8 Dimitri Gomez

www.dimitribottier.com
14 Rue Chauveau-Lagarde, 75008

Paris has a strong contingent of bespoke
shoemakers, although most are part of
bigger houses. In addition to Corthay
and Berluti, there are John Lobb Paris
(Hermès), Massaro (Chanel) and Dimitri
Gomez, who works out of Crockett &
Jones. Gomez is both good value and
recommended highly by customers for
its openness to new ideas. Also worthy of
mention are Aubercy and the recent solo
launch of Philippe Atienza.

9 Pep's

www.peps-paris.com
Passage de l'Ancre,
   223 Rue Saint-Martin, 75003

10 Antoine

www.antoine1745.com
10 Avenue de l'Opéra, 75001

Paris is blessed with two wonderful
umbrella-makers – something very few
cities have. Michel Heurtault (see pages
162–67) makes perhaps the finest in
the world, but Pep's is a much more
practical, straightforward maker offering
great value for money. Antoine, a cane
shop that has been on Avenue de l'Opéra
since 1745 and has a large selection of
umbrellas, along with an astonishing
range of gentlemen's walking sticks, is
also worth a visit.

11 Maison Bonnet

www.maisonbonnet.com
5 Rue des Petits-Champs, 75001

Maison Bonnet has a stellar reputation
for bespoke glasses, particularly for its
stock of old tortoiseshell frames, and the
boutique is a real destination for stylish
men looking for their perfect pair. There
is now a small second store in London,
but Paris has the greater range of stock
and the history.

12 Chapal
chapal.fr
244 Rue de Rivoli, 75001

13 Seraphin
www.seraphin-france.com
57 Quai de Valmy, 75010

Paris boasts some of the best makers of leather jackets in the world. Chapal is an old name that became famous for pilots' jackets from the early days of aviation (supplying Charles Lindbergh and later the French and US air forces). Ignore the jeans, T-shirts and goggles and focus on the authentically detailed 'USAAF' and 'A2' models. Seraphin is a more regular luxury brand, but produces all the leather for its jackets in Paris as well as supplying several designer labels.

14 Mes Chaussettes Rouges
www.meschaussettesrouges.com
9 Rue César Franck, 75015

Two young guys who sell – you guessed it – socks. Not just red socks, fortunately, but a large range of classic and sporting socks as well as Simonnot-Godard handkerchiefs. The shop often hosts trunk shows and other events.

15 Camille Fournet and Lavabre Cadet
www.camillefournet.com
lavabrecadet.com
5 Rue Cambon, 75001

Camille Fournet makes lovely leather watch straps – of which Paris has a surfeit, with Jean Rousseau and Atelier du Bracelet Parisien among other makers. Fournet has also taken over running the glovemaker Lavabre Cadet, and both now occupy the shop on Rue Cambon.

16 Hermès
www.hermes.com
24 Rue du Faubourg Saint-Honoré, 75008

Hermès, of course, has stores in most large cities in the world. But the flagship on Rue du Faubourg Saint-Honoré deserves a pilgrimage – rather like visiting the Armani headquarters in Milan. The flagship is a towering temple to the leather and silk specialist, with artefacts of the company's history displayed on the walls and in cases. And given how small are the runs of some pieces, there will always be something here that you haven't seen elsewhere.

Paris

ARC DE
TRIOMPHE

6

8

4 8TH ARR.

16

7 3 5

15 2

12

PLACE
VENDÔME

10

1ST ARR.

LOUVRE MUSEUM

* EIFFEL TOWER

14 14TH ARR.

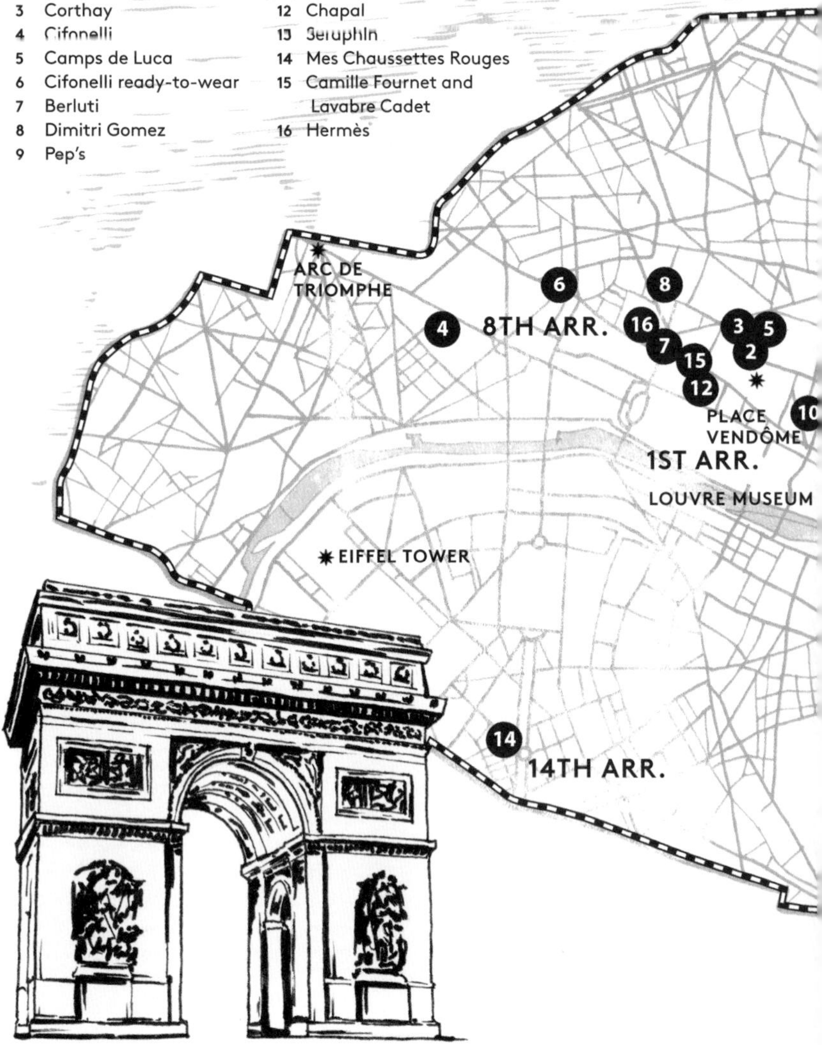

GARE DU NORD

13

9

3RD ARR.

11TH ARR.

1

Heurtault

An ex-costume maker uses his knowledge of
vintage umbrellas to create some of the most beautiful
and original examples available anywhere in the world

'The opening of the umbrella should sound like a car door,' says Michel Heurtault, looking up meaningfully. I don't get the connection immediately, but he slowly pushes the umbrella open, and when it locks there is a 'thunk' of metal sinking into wood. The resemblance to the sound of a car door closing is marked, and very satisfying.

Umbrellas are potentially beautiful accessories. The range of woods that can be used in their shafts is very broad – even today when so few 'coppiced' woods are kept for the purpose. The canopies can be made of any cotton, polyester or silk – with the latter having the most potential. The handles and ends can be made of many different precious materials – most commonly buffalo horn, and, more rarely, even gold and silver.

But men rarely get any of this. Men's umbrellas are nearly always black, with a dark wood or metal shaft and a fairly nondescript handle. Only a handful of European makers go any further and make single-stick pieces (in which the shaft and handle are made from a single piece of wood) or use unusual materials.

Other notable umbrella makers worldwide are Mario Talarico in Naples (see pages 120–23) and Francesco Maglia in Milan. The UK has James Smith & Sons and Fox, though neither has quite the artisan detail of the Italian makers.

Michel Heurtault, however, takes things to a whole new level. The Paris-based umbrella maker has been in business for only seven years, but is already renowned for bringing a fine, couture level of work even to everyday

umbrellas. For 20 years, Michel had worked in restoring and reconstructing period costumes and corsets for film and theatre – along with a stint in 1996 making haute couture for John Galliano at Dior. Then in 2008 he decided to set out on his own, bringing that vintage and couture experience to new creations.

'I learned pretty much everything I knew in the years of collecting and restoring old pieces,' he says. 'There used to be such experimentation and creativity in umbrellas and parasols, nearly all of which has been lost today. Women's parasols in particular were absolute works of art.' Much of Michel's work is for women or for costume use – including elaborate pieces with lace or hand-embroidered canopies that really show off his abilities – but he also makes many elegant and subtle men's pieces.

So what does he do with his umbrellas that's different? Well, he doesn't bend and manipulate his own woods, which is one highlight of the work at Talarico or Maglia. His wooden handles are all bought-in, pre-shaped. But the work he does with the finishing, canopy and sewing is exceptional.

Each piece of the canopy (always silk or linen, never synthetic) is cut by hand so that the patterns match perfectly – like on the shoulders

of a shirt. The circle of silk that sits inside the canopy, against the shaft, is cut with serrated scissors into a ring of points, creating a flower-like piece of silk origami. On the top of the canopy, another circle of silk is ruched up against the shaft, creating a lovely transition. 'I used to just nail a collar on at that point, but it seemed so abrupt,' Michel says. 'It was nice to be able to add a little touch of couture instead.' Applied to a dark silk canopy, these touches are very subtle and never effeminate. Many of the silks he uses for men's umbrellas come from tiemakers, so they are quite formal and geometric in their patterns.

In common with other top-end makers, Michel usually uses horn for the umbrella tip. But he also inserts horn in other places, such as in the curve of the handle. This is typical of his luxurious and inventive approach to design – which often also involves precious metals and skins. He recently incorporated a jade handle made by Fabergé for a female client.

There are many other craft points. The canopies usually have a slight wave to them, curving up as they leave the shaft and then running down towards the edge. The canopies are also sometimes lined, with a second layer of silk. And there's the way the mechanism is lined up with the shaft, creating that car-like clunk.

Michel's shop – under an archway in Paris's 12th arrondissement – is a cosy space. The back half holds a workshop for him and his apprentice, Andrea. Michel points out that handing down his skills is an explicit requirement of the Maître d'Arte award

OPPOSITE ABOVE The Heurtault shop below the arches on Avenue Daumesnil.

OPPOSITE BELOW A circle of silk ruched around the umbrella shaft by hand.

PAGE 162 The author rolls an umbrella.

he holds from the French government – it requires *'mission et remission'*.

Most of Michel's work is made to order, but there are always a handful of men's and women's umbrellas lying around either to buy or for inspiration. Most men's models start at around €490 and take anything from three days to three weeks to make, depending on the materials. Those involving precious woods are usually between €1000 and €2000.

This is, of course, extremely expensive for an umbrella. But it feels good to know there is a top-end to the spectrum of makers, from Fox through Maglia to Heurtault. And the level of work is a suitable accompaniment for a Camps de Luca suit or an Hermès briefcase.

THESE PAGES Malacca and other wooden handles on display.

Charvet

The first shirt shop in the world, and still standing after more than 180 years, Charvet has to be a destination for men seeking out the world's best clothing

Charvet is, quite simply, one of the finest houses of traditional menswear still remaining in the world.

It is stocked full of history. The first-ever dedicated shirt shop, it was founded in 1838 at a time when shirts were normally made by general wardrobe suppliers, with cloth supplied by the customer. Shirts of that era were normally made from square or rectangular pieces of cloth, with no shaping seams or shoulder yoke. The shirt was not yet a focus of male dress.

Charvet was at the forefront in changing that. It was the first place in the world where a customer could come to be measured, select a cloth and then have a shirt made to his specifications. It was also one of the first to begin shaping the shirt to the body, and is said to have invented both the turn-down collar and the detachable collar. For decades afterwards, France was the global centre of shirtmaking, and Charvet its acme. Charvet made shirts for many 19th- and 20th-century heads of state, and was the first to make ready-made shirts for export to Russia, the USA and further abroad.

With such pedigree, it is remarkable that Charvet still stands – the last of a group of great French shirtmakers and the last remaining maker on Place Vendôme, where it has occupied various addresses since 1877. If you visit Paris and have even a passing interest in menswear, you need to visit.

Walk in the front door, and the abundance of fine, bright clothing hits you like a multicoloured sun. There are racks and racks of silk neckties, in a profusion of patterns and shades – each new design usually comes in a

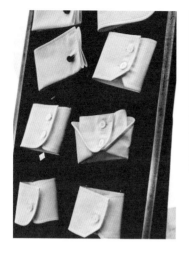

FAR LEFT Sample cuff designs.

LEFT The author being measured for a shirt.

PAGE 168 Shirt collar options on display.

couple of dozen colours. There are silk cravats, silk handkerchiefs, and silk-knot cufflinks (which Charvet, of course, invented).

It is very rare today that a fashion store offers such a wide spectrum of clothing in a single category. Usually men are offered a mere handful of options by a brand each season, and are told that this is it – this is what they should be wearing. Charvet, however, has 24 shades of knitted-silk tie on offer all the time, year in and year out – including five different shades of grey alone.

If anything, the abundance is even more impressive on the third floor (of seven), which is the home of bespoke shirtmaking. The entire floor is stacked with bolts of shirt cloth. Many of them are unique to Charvet, but even if they're not, no shop shows them in such volume, in full bolts – which can be unwound and draped across the body, to get a sense of the style at full-scale.

The master of this realm is Jean-Claude Colban, who runs Charvet with his sister Anne-Marie. (Denis Colban, their father, bought the shop in 1965 when it was being sold by the original Charvet heirs.) Ask Jean-Claude about shirt fabrics, and you dive into a world of cottons, weights and weaves – the most lasting memory of which is likely to be a discussion of the many different shades of white, and which ones have been trending for the past few years.

Charvet has suffered in recent years, most obviously from the drop in men wearing neckties, particularly bright, shiny ones. But the range of product is so great that there is always something desirable, and the bespoke shirts continue to be popular.

Charvet needs a change, and hopefully Jean-Claude and Anne-Marie are the people to do it. After all, it was their father who revolutionized Charvet in the 1960s, offering bright and patterned shirtings for the first time, and instructing staff to guide the customers, rather than dictate to them. It would be a horrible shame to see it go.

TOP AND ABOVE RIGHT Tie designs in storage.

ABOVE LEFT Collar options.

RIGHT Looking through the Charvet archive.

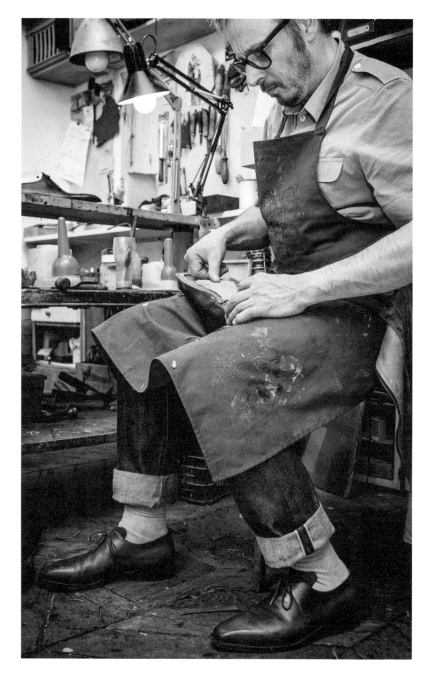

Corthay

The original home of French shoemaker Corthay is a warren of art, colour and – here and there – some beautiful shoes

If there are, broadly, three traditions in men's footwear – English, French and Italian – then the French is the least well-known, but also easily the most provocative. Characterized by strong colours and aggressive shapes, French bespoke shoes have had a tendency towards the artistic, with the makers seeing themselves as masters of an art rather than practical shodders of the French gentleman.

Pierre Corthay, who founded shoemaker Corthay after several years at Berluti, is certainly in this tradition. His bespoke and ready-to-wear collections have always included pieces in bright patent leathers, with unusual patinas or made from exotic skins such as camel and ostrich.

This aesthetic is reinforced by the decoration in Corthay's shop and bespoke atelier on Rue Volnay in Paris.

Don't be surprised to see, when you visit, sculptures made from shoes that appear to have melted together, or seem to be dripping off the shelf. They will all be made in the same way as a normal bespoke shoe – with upper, lining and sole all stitched together – just distorted for effect. Despite all these flights of fancy, however, you will also discover some beautiful and highly wearable shoes. Pierre's genius has always been creating last shapes that appear quite long or extreme in shape, but remain (relatively) wearable.

Classic models like the 'Arca', for instance, have a long front ending in a rather square toe, with the length accentuated by a simple two-hole fastening across the top. The 'Wilfrid' – another classic and one of my personal favourites – has a rounded toe but,

if anything, an even longer profile, usually with a suede section around the laces.

It is on models like the 'Wilfrid' that you will often see the best examples of patina work on Corthay shoes. Many brands now offer a hand-painted patina, but Corthay was one of the first, after Berluti, to do so at this level in France. The subtle blending of colours in a hand-painted leather patina, often built up in layers over several hours, can truly be called a work of art – and can lead Corthay customers to become obsessive about protecting their shoes from scuffs and the errant boots of others on the streets of Paris.

The Corthay buildings combine a ready-to-wear shop, offices and bespoke workshops. Even if you don't plan to buy a pair of bespoke shoes immediately, it is worth visiting for a tour of the workshops both upstairs and down, with the stacks of leather stored under one underground arch, and the wooden lasts hanging in another.

As well as shoes, Corthay offers a range of distinctive leather goods, including wallets and belts. Both display the same superb patina work, and the belt buckles, with a sweeping 'C' on the front in a variety of metals, offer a subtler alternative to the big buckles of Hermès or Gucci.

Although Corthay shoes are now available around the world, the original shop in Paris is the most characterful and certainly worth a visit.

Stockholm

Swedes may be the best-dressed men on earth. At their best, they combine the classicism of the English with the flair of the Italians – without the stuffiness of the former or showiness of the latter. Although young Swedes today are heavily influenced by Italy – soft tailoring, turn-ups, *sprezzatura* – they usually avoid that extra touch of flamboyance, or gaudiness, to which Italian style can be susceptible. Stockholm is a wonderful city to visit and in which to shop. It has never had the range of menswear stores of London, Milan or New York, but what's there is always tasteful and well done. In common with many capital cities around the world, Stockholm has also seen the opening of a number of new, sartorially focused boutiques in recent years.

The List

1 Skoaktiebolaget

www.skoaktiebolaget.se
Nybrogatan 23, 114 39

See Brand Focus on pages 186–89.

2 A. W. Bauer

journal.awbauer.com
Brunnsgatan 4, 111 38

See Brand Focus on pages 190–95.

3 Gabucci

www.gabucci.se
Nybrogatan 14, 114 39

Founded in 1994, Gabucci is a multi-brand store selling both casual and formal Italian brands – Attolini and Caruso alongside Boglioli and Aspesi.

It also offers its own-brand tailoring, and is one of the best places in the city for advice on suits. The men's shop moved location a few years ago, into a large, lovely space with room to express the formal and casual sides of the offering.

4 Lund & Lund

www.lundochlund.se
Sturegatan 12, 114 36

Like many smaller European cities, Stockholm's high-end menswear mostly used to consist of stores selling Italian tailoring (Kiton, Brioni) and some very English knitwear or accessories. Lund & Lund was the most famous of these stores, founded as a tailor in 1949 and branching out into ready-to-

1

2

6 Herr Judit

www.herrjudit.se
Hornsgatan 65, 08-658 30 37

A great vintage menswear store, with everything from Rubinacci to Hermès and Incotex, it has especially nice accessories, bags and ties.

7 Rose & Born

www.roseborn.com
Grevgatan 2, 114 53

A more high-street Swedish brand compared to many shops included here, but certainly recommended on the strength of its young, sartorial outlook, style, and level of taste.

wear clothing in 1963. It is still owned and run by the same family, and the internal decor hasn't changed much. It stocks Belvest, Cucinelli, with a made-to-measure service from Caruso, Corneliani and others.

5 Hans Allde

www.hansallde.se
Birger Jarlsgatan 58, 114 29

Similar to Lund & Lund, with a history going back to 1949, this multi-brand shop stocks Zegna, Corneliani, Belvest and Kiton. It also has an in-house bespoke tailor, Annika Hedh, alongside made-to-measure from the Italian brands.

8 Tweed Country Sports

www.countrysports.se
Odengatan 98, 113 22

Tweed reminds me of the odd store you find in Italy that is clearly obsessed with English style and English products. It stocks mid-range Dent's gloves, Corgi socks and the likes of Magee and Chrysalis.

9 A. Marchesan

www.facebook.com amarchesanstockholm
amarchesan.se
Odengatan 74, 113 24

Another vintage men's store, with a large selection of 1940s/50s suits, hats and accessories. Its atmosphere is rather different to that of Herr Judit, but certainly worth a visit.

1

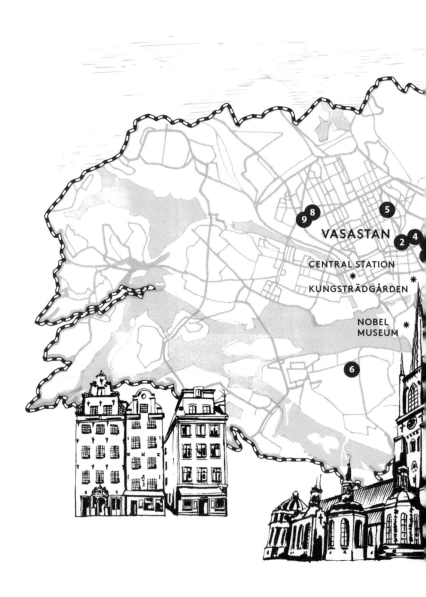

VASASTAN

CENTRAL STATION
*

KUNGSTRÄDGÅRDEN
*

NOBEL
MUSEUM *

Stockholm

ERMALM

Skoaktiebolaget

A local shoe store with an international reach, Skoaktiebolaget has come to cater to some of the most obsessive shoe buyers in the world – many of whom, it turns out, are in Sweden

Men who are into their clothing often spend a surprising amount of money on shoes. The twin attractions of long-lasting quality and dapper aesthetics make spending £1000 or more on a pair of oxfords perfectly justifiable. Patrik Löf, co-founder of Swedish store Skoaktiebolaget ('Skoak' for short) set up his shop in 2012 to cater to just this type of local enthusiast. 'Stockholm was so poorly served for men's shoes – with just Church's and Crockett & Jones in town – that I felt there had to be an opportunity there,' he says.

Löf's background is in IT, and he still runs his own business-to-business IT company with Skoak co-founder Daniel Tung. The plan was for the two of them to finance the new store, and have friend Adam Kruse manage it. But Kruse tragically died before the store could open, pushing Löf into the front line and managing it from day one.

'It wasn't how any of us would have wanted things to start, but we're back on track now,' says Löf. 'We have a large new shop and a great team, which means I'm stepping back from the day-to-day running.'

Skoak specializes in handmade footwear – classic men's shoes, often hand-sewn, finished and polished by small makers from around Europe. There is Enzo Bonafé, a family-run Italian company that was started in 1963, which offers some unusual models such as grey-and-black button boots alongside classic Balmoral oxfords and several models in cordovan (horse leather).

The UK is represented by John Lobb (the ready-to-wear brand owned by Hermès, different from the

LEFT Founders Patrik Löf and Daniel Tung.

BELOW Tassel loafers on display.

OPPOSITE The interior, with stacked shoe boxes as decoration.

PAGE 186 Shoes on display in a shop window overlooking Nybrogatan.

family-owned original bespoke makers on St James's Street in London), which does beautiful Northampton-made classics. Styles include cap toes and wing-tips in a variety of blacks and browns, and many made in the company's well-known 'museum calf' leather, which gives the shoe an aged and dappled look.

Skoaktiebolaget ('Shoe, Incorporated' in Swedish) also carries a large range of shoe-care products, alongside socks and knitted ties from Italian maker Sozzi and ties and scarves from Neapolitan maker Rubinacci.

The new store, with big windows looking down on Nybrogatan in central Stockholm, is a wonderful space to display such accessories and clothing. The old shop, though cosy, was only enough for a few racks of shoes. Now a long central table displays the staff's favourite selection of models, and boxes in the walls rise up to the high ceiling.

Since Skoak opened, Löf has seen a consistently strong local response from both young enthusiasts and an older, professional class. 'There

was a local demand here that had been bottled up, waiting for a store like this,' he says. 'We're still not that widely known around Sweden, but the connoisseurs quickly knew and they have been very faithful. We're shoe geeks just like them.'

And just as rewarding for Löf is the knowledge that the store is helping to preserve traditional European craft. 'For decades these specialists have seen their business steadily decline – meaning they couldn't afford to hire staff, or keep training young people. Finally, in the past 10 years, that has started to turn around. It's great to be a part of it – however small.'

A. W. Bauer

An old Swedish name with a bright future – thanks to two young and very enthusiastic bespoke tailors

In recent years there has been a groundswell of young people training as tailors, particularly in Europe and Japan. On Savile Row there hasn't been such an influx of new talent for 40 years. In Sweden, an example of this trend is A. W. Bauer & Co. in Stockholm, founded 150 years ago and now owned and run by Frederik Andersen and Martin Ekolin, two young tailors who have revitalized what was pretty much the last bespoke brand in the country.

The Bauer store is just off the busy Birger Jarlsgatan, with a ground-floor entrance. It has a small shop in the front and workrooms behind glass doors at the back.

Frederik, the cutter, has an unusual background. He started off as an apprentice in the theatre, making costumes. Although he says

that theatrical costume-making is rather looked down upon by most tailors, it does give a broad technical grounding, and the costumes require a surprisingly high-quality make given the rigours they have to endure over a long run.

The story of Frederik's transition to full bespoke is one of perseverance. He was originally dismissed out of hand when he first came to Bauer looking for work. But he came back a month later, and eventually managed to convince the owner, Börje Moberg, to let him come in every Friday afternoon.

There were only three people working at Bauer by that point – including Moberg – and they were all old. A few months after Frederik started at Bauer, Moberg said they were going to close up. 'He didn't

think there was any future in tailoring. Bauer was the only full tailor in Sweden and demand was dwindling,' recalls Frederik. 'He said "No one understands bespoke, and we're sick of explaining it to people."'

Fortunately, Frederik convinced Moberg to let him and Martin purchase the business by slowly buying up the shares, and eventually taking on all new customers while Moberg continued to work with his old ones. That was 12 years ago, and four years ago Moberg retired fully, leaving Frederik and Martin in charge.

Since then, business has been strong. The team is now up to six people in-house and two off-site, and Frederik and Martin have even started a small school, taking on the best people to train as tailors. 'As you might expect, we get a lot more enthusiasts into the shop now, people who really understand the product,' says Frederik. 'These things are so much easier with social media, and people are fascinated by it.'

It's hard not to feel impressed and grateful that – 150 years after it first opened, and at a time when it was about to close – Frederik and Martin have managed to give the last fully bespoke firm in Sweden a new and bright future.

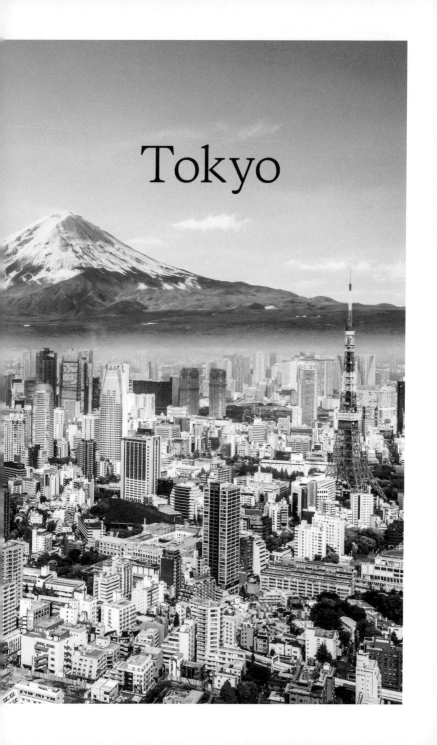

Tokyo

Shopping in Tokyo is arguably the most varied, creative and stimulating retail experience in the world. Not only is the city huge, but each area has a distinctive feel and atmosphere. I recommend grouping the shops listed here (which are only a starting point, as there are so many) into areas, since the size of Tokyo means it can take a while to get from one area to another. There are small, niche brands everywhere, as well as workshops and artisanal ateliers – and, surprisingly, some of the bespoke makers operate out of Japanese department stores. Many of the others work in small upstairs studios, without a street-level storefront, and usually don't offer ready-to-wear, so you should try to make an appointment in advance. But once in an area, whether glitzy Ginza or funky Daikanyama, take the time to wander around and see what else pops out. You might step into Tsutaya Books, for example, and end up whiling away most of an afternoon.

The List

1 Bryceland's Co
www.brycelandsco.com
1F J-Hillside Building, 3-15-4 Jingumae, Shibuya-ku

See Brand Focus, pages 204–07.

2 Motoji
www.motoji.co.jp
3-8-15 Ginza, Chuo-ku

See Brand Focus, pages 208–13.

3 Sartoria Ciccio
www.ciccio.co.jp
5-4-43 Minami Aoyama, Minato-ku

See Brand Focus, pages 214–17.

4 Isetan
isetan.mistore.jp
3-14-1 Shinjuku, Shinjuku-ku

Department stores in Japan do things very well, from the brand mix to the merchandising. But the thing that sets them apart for most is the prominence of bespoke and made-to-measure clothing from all around the world. Isetan's Shinjuku flagship is worth seeing for the pure department store experience, but also make sure to visit the made-to-measure area, and look out for any trunk shows going on at the time. Oh, and there's a whole building just for menswear.

5 Strasburgo
strasburgo.co.jp
3-18-1 Minami Aoyama, Minato-ku

Strasburgo takes the menswear focus a step further, with a more select range, and a more sartorial approach than the other department stores. It has several branches around the city; I recommend the Minami Aoyama store, for both its ready-to-wear selection and the Tailor's Lab that was established on the third floor a few years ago. There you will find a workshop housing artisans such as shirtmaker Masanori Yamagami and tailor Noriyuki Higashi (Sartoria Domenica). Trouser-maker Toru Igarashi also started out here.

2

6 Beams F and International Gallery Beams

www.beams.co.jp
Beams F: 1F/2F, 3-25-14 Jingumae,
    Shibuya-ku
International Gallery Beams: B1F/1F/2F,
    3-25-15 Jingumae, Shibuya-ku

Beams is a smaller, more curated store (or rather, series of stores) and is worth visiting for its level of taste and comprehensive selection of great American and European brands. It's sad how many great Italian brands, for example, don't get stockists in London. New York is better, but Tokyo is the best. The two sister stores mentioned here are both worth a visit: Beams F for sartorial European brands, and International Gallery Beams next door for casual and designer clothing.

7 Yohei Fukuda

yoheifukuda.tumblr.com
BAL Aoyama 2F, 2-12-27 Kitaaoyama,
    Minato-ku

8 Marquess

marquess-bespoke.blogspot.jp
8F Ginza Yurika Building, 1-19-3 Ginza,
    Chuo-ku

Japan has a huge number of bespoke shoemakers, perhaps more than the whole of Europe combined. They are largely young, working in small workshops and offering good value for money – though waiting times can be long. Most importantly, the quality of their work is amazing, often beating that of the European masters who trained them. There are so many good shoemakers in Tokyo to try, but it is certainly worth visiting Yohei Fukuda and Shoji Kawaguchi, the latter operating under the brand Marquess.

9 Igarashi

igarashitrousers.jp
2-31-9 Jingumae, Shibuya-ku

10 Osaku

www.m059.net
7-10-6 Ikuta, Tama-ku

It is worth highlighting two of the excellent Japanese workshops that make only bespoke trousers: Toru Igarashi and Hayato Osaku. Igarashi is located in the centre of Tokyo and is therefore the easier of the two to visit. Osaku works from a small town an hour's drive outside of the city, but comes into the centre for appointments. Their work displays a high level of precision in details such as curved waistbands and neat pick stitching.

11 Ortus

www.ortus-bag.com
2F, 1-24-5 Ginza, Chuo-ku

Among all the bespoke menswear craftsmen listed here, leather master Naoyuki Komatsu probably has the most stellar reputation. He runs a small workshop called Ortus, which does 90% bespoke pieces such as day bags and wallets. Everything is entirely hand-sewn; Komatsu even goes so far as to make the brass hardware, which are small works of beauty in themselves. A signature design is the 'music bag' – a briefcase made of one piece of leather with a brass bar securing the single handle.

12 Okura

www.hrm.co.jp/okura
20-11 Sarugaku-cho, Shibuya-ku

Shifting our focus to workwear, Okura is a great shop for anyone who loves indigo-dyed clothing, another traditional

Japanese technique. Located in the Daikanyama area, it is stocked floor-to-ceiling with indigo-dyed jackets, T-shirts, sweatshirts and kimonos, both from domestic brands like Blue Blue Japan and cheaper versions made abroad. Look out for pieces in sashiko cloth in particular.

13 UES

ues.co.jp
Abiadaikanyama Building #101, 26-7 Sarugaku, Shibuya-ku

Around the corner from Okura in Daikanyama is a tiny outlet of UES, part of whose mission is to avoid waste – by making classic garments (both American and traditional Japanese styles) that last, and then encouraging customers to repair and re-use them. (The word 'ues' is a Japanese pronunciation of 'waste'.) Specialist pieces include Western shirts, deck jackets, chinos and T-shirts made from a mix of standard organic cotton and Desi cotton. Make sure to take advice on sizing, as pieces can be either 'shrink to fit' or made to grow out with wear.

14 Ring Jacket

www.ringjacket.co.jp
14a Ginza store: 6-10-1 Ginza, Chuo-ku
14b Aoyama store: 5-5-4 Minami Aoyama, Minato-ku

Ring Jacket is the first Japanese tailoring brand to have achieved serious recognition around the world, largely thanks to the promotion of The Armoury in Hong Kong and New York (see pages 54–59, 135). There are two stores in Tokyo, in Ginza and Aoyama, and the brand is also stocked in Isetan (see above).

The style is Italian and soft-shouldered, although there is a range of models (a decent reason to visit one of the stand-alone stores rather than just Isetan) and they also offer accessories and leather goods, all with rather Italian styling as well. The tailoring is well made and good value, particularly in Japan compared to imported Italian brands.

15 Arts & Science

www.arts-science.com
Aoyama store: 105 Palace Aoyama, 6-1-6 Minami Aoyama, Minato-ku

Arts & Science is a small chain of stores in Tokyo founded by stylist Sonya Park. It is an interesting crossover between Japanese crafts and modern, minimal sensibilities, with accessories, menswear and womenswear.

Although the clothing offering is pretty small, it is a good place to find unusual (if expensive) homewares and accessories, in simple styles and colours. Look out for loose linen jackets, wooden boxes and leather pouches. We recommend both the Aoyama and Daikanyama branches.

1

SHINJUKU

4

9 AOY.

5–7

1

3

SHIBUYA

14b

15

12

13

10

Tokyo

CHIYODA

✳ IMPERIAL PALACE

✳ HIMBASHI STATION

✳ TOKYO TOWER

8
2 11
14a
CHUO
GINZA

Bryceland's Co

A combination of traditional workwear
and classic tailoring give this store, founded
by Ethan Newton, a distinctive outlook

Bryceland's created quite a stir when
it first opened in Tokyo in 2016, given
the following that Australian founder
Ethan Newton had established in his
years at cult store The Armoury in
Hong Kong. Many, including myself,
were intrigued to see how he would
combine his two loves: classic tailoring
and casual Americana.

The results are interesting and
unique. The tailoring is essentially a
soft Italian make from Neapolitans
such as Dalcuore and Orazio Luciano,
but in distinctive English cloths:
heavy hopsacks and coverts, all solid
and hard-wearing. The cut has been
tweaked to Ethan's style in several
areas: a broad chest, small waist and
larger sleeve in the jacket, with a high-
waisted, full-legged trouser.

'This is a man's cut – a big chest
and a strong arm. It's something not

all customers understand at first,
but it's very intuitive when you start
talking about it,' says Ethan. His
camel overcoat from Orazio has been
similarly tweaked, with more belly
on the lapel and a lower gorge. 'I
wouldn't say the tailoring draws on one
particular era, but there are certainly
influences from the 1920s and into the
1930s,' adds Ethan.

Ethan had some training in
tailoring when he was in Australia,
and is trying to improve today with the
help of Japanese tailor Yusuche Ono,
known as Anglofilo, who has a studio
in the back of the shop. 'My pattern-
making is getting pretty good now,'
Ethan says, 'but my making is still
pretty terrible.'

The shop also sells ready-made
trousers cut by Neapolitan tailor
Salvatore Ambrosi (see page 117), who

antique chain-stitching and button-hole machines.

There is clearly a big market for Americana and vintage clothing in Japan, but does that also mean there is a lot of competition? 'In some ways yes, but actually the market here has become very narrow,' says Ethan. 'Everyone just wants the iconic pieces – the 1955 501s, for example. There aren't many people offering something different.' Bryceland's co-founder Kenji Cheung gets some credit for identifying this gap in the Japanese vintage/Americana market.

One aspect of Ethan's approach that is particularly appealing is his emphasis on value. He likes brands like Alden and Saint Crispin's because they offer such great value for money, and he tries to sell things at a fair price (without ever going on sale). This is one reason he has Bryceland's shirts made at Ascot Chang in Hong Kong – they are well made, and much more reasonably priced than those imported from Italy.

It is also important to Ethan that Bryceland's pieces wear well and are made to last. 'It links to the appeal of vintage, for me – the idea that these new clothes we're selling could also go on to be great vintage in the future,' says Ethan.

also visits for trunk shows. The fit of the ready-made trousers is interesting, with a higher rise in the back than in the front. The range isn't big, but Ethan's skill with fitting makes made-to-measure an attractive option.

Bryceland's dress shirts, often in unusual patterns and stripes, are made to Ethan's cut and specifications by Ascot Chang (see page 50) with a full body and nice roll to the collar. The ties are made by Kenji Kaga's Sevenfold brand (also known as Tie Your Tie) in nice, muted, classic colours.

On the workwear side, Ethan has a lot of nice vintage pieces – which are one-offs and expensive – alongside some re-created ranges such as jeans that mimic 1947 Levi's 501s, made by a local Japanese maker using

ABOVE A Bryceland's camel overcoat.

OPPOSITE Craft is always visible in-store, particularly when Salvatore Ambrosi (centre left) is making impromptu alterations.

PAGE 204 Founder Ethan Newton.

Motoji

By promoting the finest homegrown cloth, and educating the wider public, storied kimono house Motoji is reinvigorating a traditional Japanese craft

In the world of menswear, silk is usually restricted to discussions of ties and handkerchiefs. There is the occasional silk facing and silk-mix jacketing, but it rarely features alone in clothing. When travelling in Japan it can therefore be interesting to learn a bit about the prominent use of silk in traditional Japanese dress for men.

Although fitting and tailoring is important in making a high-quality Japanese kimono, the real focus is the cloth. The craft is all about harvesting the best silks, specialist dyeing using natural pigments and traditional processes, and then employing a variety of small-scale weaving techniques to create different shapes and spectacular effects in the woven silk.

Motoji, in the Ginza region of Tokyo, is one of the most famous kimono houses in the country. It uses silk farmed in Japan (which represents only 1% of the global production – most comes from China or Brazil) and employs only local tailors, rather than outsourcing the work to China or Vietnam.

Traditional kimono silks have details of the cloth and of its makers printed on notes at the end of the bolt, and at Motoji there is a particular emphasis on naming the weaver of the silk. 'Putting the name on the cloth elevates the importance of the weaver,' says Keita Motoji, son of founder Komei Motoji. 'It makes them famous, at least in our world, and they will often come to the shop to have a photograph taken next to the cloth with their name on it.'

That level of recognition also helps to encourage apprentice weavers to take up the trade, and to keep it going across generations. And, as elsewhere in the world, there is a resurgence in the recognition of the importance of crafts, although Japan has always maintained a strong tradition of valuing handmade products as art.

One cloth example is accompanied by a leaflet about how it was dyed: in the north of Japan, on the island of Hokkaido, because the water used to extract one of the dyes from a particular type of flower has to be cold and fresh. These flowers are picked in the summer when they bloom, but are only used for the dyeing in the winter – and even then, the work must be done before dawn to ensure that the water is as cold as possible.

Keita periodically hosts demonstrations of silk farming to increase appreciation of traditional Japanese textiles. In an adjoining shop, he suspends thousands of silkworm cocoons in racks from the ceiling. Around 3,000 cocoons (from male silkworms, which make longer fibres) are required to make 1 metre of cloth. Keita invites groups of schoolchildren to come and play with the silkworms, and to show them to passers-by.

'When I was younger I hated the shop, and kimonos', says Keita. 'All I wanted was Western clothes. But

OPPOSITE One of many beautiful finished kimono on display.

OVERLEAF A kimono fastened tightly at the waist with a traditional knot.

PAGE 208 Komei Motoji.

ABOVE Silkworm (top) and silk (above).

RIGHT AND ABOVE RIGHT Selecting fabric for a kimono.

over time I learned to love it, and now I'm passionate about trying to spread awareness of it around Japan.'

The process of being fitted for a kimono is also interesting. It is different from a fitting for a Western bespoke suit in that the focus is on the drape: how the cloth is held and tied in order to help it hang in very precise ways. Different materials – light and heavy silks, linens, cottons (usually for summer yukata) – drape very differently, so the selection of the right cloth is crucial.

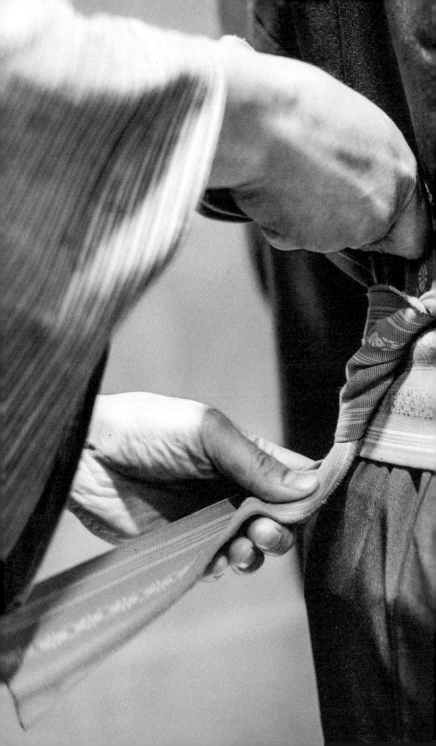

Sartoria Ciccio

**The best known of Tokyo's new crop of bespoke tailors
combines the style of Italy with the precision of Japan**

Noriyuki Ueki, founder of Sartoria Ciccio, has become the best known of a new wave of Japanese bespoke tailors who have gone to Italy in the past 20 years, trained, and returned to Japan.

Like that of many of these Italian-trained tailors, Ueki's style is soft: Neapolitan, but with a Japanese focus on precise details and execution. 'It's always the small things that get me excited', he says. 'Like the smooth run of a jacket's shoulder up into the neck. It's not hard to get the basic things right – the size of a lapel, the run down through the waist – but the harder, subtler points are what set apart good tailoring for me.'

Ueki started his career at Japanese ready-to-wear suit factory Ring Jacket, as did many of his peers in this new generation. He joined in 2000 and was

there for five years, before travelling to Naples to look for an apprenticeship. 'I wanted to go to Naples because I was impressed by the softness of the tailoring I had seen come back to Japan,' he says, 'And I knew that Ono-san [renowned Japanese tailor Yusuche Ono, known as "Anglofilo"] had gone.'

Like most other Japanese apprentices, he knew little about Naples, but simply turned up and hoped for the best. Ueki ended up at Sartoria Dalcuore, where he worked for 18 months, and then moved to Sartoria Pascariello, where he stayed for another two years.

He gained the nickname 'Ciccio' while in Italy. A shortening of 'Francesco', the name of several respected tailors in the past, it was given to him partly in recognition of the quality of his work.

After Ueki returned to Japan, he was for a long time the in-house tailor for Japanese brand Tie Your Tie, renting a space upstairs from the shop. But after seven years, he felt he had enough business to set out on his own. He opened the new atelier in 2015 in a large space down a semi-residential street, with lots of natural light. The atelier now has four other cutters and coat-makers.

'Business has been good, steady', he says – with the first suggestion of a smile on a face that is otherwise still and attentive. 'We make nine or ten suits a month, and there has been some nice press.' Ueki now travels in Asia, to Seoul and to The Armoury in Hong Kong, as well as elsewhere in Japan.

He makes a lot of sports jackets, something that is obvious from the rack of fittings waiting along one side of the shop when we visited. 'That seems to have happened recently', he says. 'We had some lovely Kiton jacketings that we were offering for a while, but sports jackets are just more suited to modern men at work – even in formal Japan.'

It's also fair to say that Ciccio attracts a young clientele, who are often well-informed about both the nature of bespoke and the traditions of Naples. 'I have to say, I am optimistic about the bespoke trade in Japan. I'm 38, and there are a lot of tailors my age who are pushing the industry forward,' he says. 'The only issue is that there is a big gap between us and the previous generation, who are all in their seventies.'

Interestingly, Japan was about ten years ahead of Europe in its tailoring revival: the young tailors coming through on Savile Row are largely younger than Ueki, and old guard often in their sixties.

'Japan also had an issue with men retiring early, at sixty, and then not needing suits anymore,' adds Ueki. 'That led to a lot of old tailors losing their clients.'

Although Ueki doesn't want the Ciccio name to live on after him, he is concerned about providing a strong foundation for tailoring in Japan.

'I'm trying to train young people where I can, but because there are so few tailors who are 40 to 60 years old, there aren't many who are able to take on a large staff,' he says. 'The biggest difficulty is paying apprentices a decent wage when you're still small.'

Ciccio charges 580,000 yen as a starting price for a suit, and the waiting time is not long. First fittings take place two to three months after the initial order, with a second fitting around a month later.

Ciccio also works with shoemaker Hidetaka Fukaya (known as 'Il Micio'), a Japanese artisan living in Florence. His shoes are on display in the sartoria.

ABOVE The distinctive soft roll of a Ciccio jacket.

BELOW LEFT A craftsman takes a break.

BELOW RIGHT Shoes from Il Micio.

PAGE 214 Founder Noriyuki Ueki, better known as 'Ciccio'.

Great Shops
in Fifteen
Other Cities

1. AMSTERDAM

Pauw Mannen

pauw.com/en/men
**Van Baerlestraat 88-90, 1071 BB
  Amsterdam, Netherlands**

Founded after the Second World War, Dutch multi-brand store Pauw Mannen, better known simply as 'Pauw', began in womenswear, where it was the first in the Netherlands to stock fashion brands such as Kenzo and Dries Van Noten – and later expanded into menswear, becoming the first to introduce Kiton, Brioni and Loro Piana. Europe is littered with multi-brand menswear stores that have failed to adapt to the modern age. Founded by stylish local men, these stores prospered until the brands they stocked decided to open their own shops and customers drifted towards the full-brand experience. Pauw, however, responded by adding smaller makers such as Common Projects, Zanone and Ten C, and also started a successful private-label tailoring service. Today it has three menswear stores in Amsterdam and others throughout the Netherlands.

2. ATLANTA

Sid Mashburn

www.sidmashburn.com
**1198 Howell Mill Road, Suite 110,
  Atlanta, GA 30318, USA**

Founded in Atlanta, Sid Mashburn was a local menswear store that slowly became a regional specialist, and now has stores in Atlanta, Houston, Dallas, Los Angeles and Washington DC. Its eponymous founder Mashburn has been successful at maintaining the original character of the brand across those stores, and his easy-going, slightly whimsical approach to classic menswear is a refreshing one. 'If you can only have one suit, start with one the colour of the night sky', he will advise customers in his writing, or 'You know the thing about a dress shirt – it's a sport shirt waiting to happen. Take off your tie, roll up your sleeves, and that's it.' The clothing on offer runs the full gamut from suits to sneakers.

3. AUCKLAND
Crane Brothers
crane-brothers.com
**2–4 High Street, Auckland, 1010,
New Zealand**

Murray Crane is famous in New Zealand as a tailoring ambassador, pushing suits and sports jackets in a country dominated by the great outdoors and highly functional clothing. As a child, such was his obsession with tailored clothing that he was known to wear suits even when a school uniform was not required. Today Crane Brothers operates stores in Auckland, Wellington, Christchurch and Sydney; the Auckland branch is the best known. Made-to-measure tailoring is its focus, with other brands such as Drake's also on offer, and a growing line of custom-made footwear.

4. BEIJING
Brio
www.instagram.com/briobeijing
**Building 3, 8 Xindong Rd, Chaoyang
District, Beijing, China**

Although China has been growing furiously as a destination for luxury brands over the past 20 years, domestic consumers have only recently started to move away from big labels and seek out the craft-oriented side of menswear. Brio, founded by tailoring connoisseur George Wang, has taken full advantage of this trend, becoming the reference point for any artisanal brand looking to establish itself in China. Many of its brands come from Italy – Stefano Bemer shoes, Avino shirts and Ambrosi trousers – but it also stocks the likes of Begg & Co scarves and Baudoin & Lange slippers, and hosts a full range of visiting bespoke tailors.

5. BRUSSELS

Degand
www.degand.be
**Avenue Louise 415,
1050 Brussels, Belgium**

Degand is from a previous generation, compared to the independent menswear stores that have opened in the past decade. Sprawling across multiple buildings and floors, it is broad in its range of categories and styles, stocking everything from classic Italian designers offering unstructured tailoring and cashmere sweaters, to artisanal French jewellers and American belt-buckle makers. Fortunately, following a programme of refurbishment in 2017, the store has been redesigned for a new generation and is gradually being rediscovered by young and knowledgeable shoppers.

6. CHICAGO

Optimo
optimo.com
**51 W. Jackson Boulevard, Chicago,
IL 60604, USA**

One of the greatest hat stores in the world, Optimo was founded by Graham Thompson as a continuation of the work of his teacher and mentor Johnny Tyus, who ran Johnny's Hats in the city. Optimo is one of a very small number of places today offering a comprehensive set of styles, in a beautiful shop, and doing its own production. Thompson brings a youthful and modern sensibility to his hats without resorting to bright colours and exaggerated shapes. His style is classic, but manifestly relevant to a modern man. (Also worth checking out in Chicago is the second store of top-end shoe shop Leffot, whose other branch is in New York – see pages 144–49.)

7. GOTHENBURG

Linnégatan 2

www.linnegatan2.com
**Linnégatan 2, 413 04,
Gothenburg, Sweden**

The sense of style in Sweden is so strong
that some of Europe's best menswear
shops are in its smaller cities such as
Gothenburg and Malmö. Even with their
relatively small populations, such places
always have a beautifully curated local
store offering well-made menswear
that mixes the best of contemporary
and classic styles. A good example is
Linnégatan 2 in Gothenburg. Named
after its street address, the store stocks
Italian brands such as Boglioli and
Incotex alongside the best of crafted
British names including Drake's and
Private White. It also features new, up-
and-coming brands such as shirtmaker
100 Hands, which is based in Amsterdam
but makes its shirts in northern India to
an extremely high standard.

8. HANOVER

Michael Jondral

en.michaeljondral.com
Theaterstrasse 13, 30159,
 Hanover, Germany

Founded in 2006, Michael Jondral has become one of the best-respected men's haberdashers in Germany over the past 10 years. Jondral himself had been working in menswear for 20 years before he set up his own shop, motivated by a desire to bring Neapolitan style – first Kiton, and later Attolini and others – to Germany. Today he stocks everything from English hats (Lock & Co.) to French handkerchiefs (Simonnot-Godard) as well as Italian clothing and footwear from around the country.

9. LOS ANGELES

Magasin

www.magasinthestore.com
**8810 Washington Blvd #101,
Culver City, CA 90232, USA**

Founded by ex-Bloomingdale's buyer Josh Peskowitz, Magasin is a store clearly run by someone who knows the industry well, but is enjoying expressing himself by including small, boutique brands alongside bigger names. So as well as stocking Dries Van Noten and Engineered Garments, Magasin sells small brands such as Harris Wharf London and The Lost Explorer. The latter makes simple clothes in a small range of naturally dyed, sustainable fabrics, and was founded by Los Angeles-based explorer David de Rothschild.

10. MADRID

Burgos

www.camiseriaburgos.com
Calle de Cedaceros 2, 28014 Madrid, Spain

Burgos is a historic shirtmaker, with a rich history of serving the Spanish royal family, bullfighters and international celebrities such as Orson Welles and Cary Grant. The shop is beautiful, and worth a visit even if you're not interested in (or have the time for) commissioning a bespoke shirt. On that point, Burgos now offers a strong made-to-measure programme for shirts, which is rather more affordable at €80 a shirt. The programme also includes the classic Spanish 'Teba' jacket, an iconic design for the shop and very versatile given its soft, unlined construction. Elsewhere in Madrid, there are a few small tailors worth visiting, such as the excellent Calvo de Mora and Langa, where shirtmaker Mariano also works.

11. MANILA

Signet

www.instagram.com/thesignetstore

**Retail Unit GF3, Shangri-La at the Fort,
30th Street (corner 5th Avenue),
Bonifacio Global City,
Taguig 1634, Philippines**

Signet in the Philippines is very open about being inspired by independent menswear stores elsewhere in the world. But while it carries some similar products, with the same quality and the same heritage, its offering is considerably broader, encompassing casual, rugged clothing alongside the finest tailoring and footwear: Resolute and Boncoura from Japan, for example, and European brands such as Sunspel. The shop is also big on service, with founders Kelly See, Edie Lim and Jason Qua usually in store every day, talking to regulars and wearing the clothes they stock – each in their own distinctive fashion.

12. MUNICH

Lodenfrey

www.lodenfrey.com

Maffeistrasse 7, Munich 80333, Germany

Lodenfrey is a large store in the heart of Munich that has managed to maintain a reputation for classic, quality men's and women's clothing, while adding younger and more trend-driven lines in recent years. Spread across six floors, it has a loyal local following and a range of men's brands that includes Armani, Cucinelli, Ralph Lauren and Brioni. The made-to-measure suiting has a particularly strong reputation. For smaller and more classic menswear, Ed Meier in Munich is worth a visit. Originally a shoemaker, it now also offers clothing and accessories.

13. NEWCASTLE

End

www.endclothing.com
133–137 Grainger Street, Newcastle Upon Tyne, NE1 5AE, UK

End was founded in 2005 in Newcastle, in the north-east of England, to offer the city high-quality men's clothing – largely streetwear and fashion, but with some heritage, classic brands such as Alden, Barbour and Church's. What set End apart was its online store, launched a year later and now one of the biggest online men's sites in the world. The original physical store is still worth seeing though, particularly as the range of brands has expanded and its size has allowed it to offer regular exclusives.

14. SINGAPORE

Kevin Seah

kevinseah.com
The Mill, 5 Jalan Kilang, #03-01, Singapore 159405

For the past ten years, Kevin Seah's space in Singapore has been the local outpost for bespoke crafts and visiting craftsmen such as Japanese eyewear-maker Nackymade or bespoke shoemaker Masaru Okuyama. Also a keen watch and cigar enthusiast, Seah often brings a contemporary fashion-orientated approach to his clothing, with large lapels and strong patterns. A good example is his collaboration with French graffiti artist Ceet, who created a print that was used in Kevin Seah-branded sports jackets.

15. VIENNA

Wilhelm Jungmann und Neffe

www.feinestoffe.at
Albertinaplatz 3, 1010 Vienna, Austria

Wilhelm Jungmann und Neffe is a stunning shop in the centre of Vienna that has been catering to well-tailored men since 1881. It is best known locally for its fabrics, some produced in Austria and others imported from England and Italy. Several bespoke tailors operating in Prague, Bratislava and Budapest visit the shop to cater to clients. For most, however, the accessories will be the chief attraction. The cashmere scarves and shawls are available in 15–20 colours and a similar number of patterns, from the basic to the funky. This is a personally edited and often locally sourced collection, which makes it worth visiting for someone from London, Milan or Paris. The madder ties, for example, are made by a company just outside Vienna – the only maker outside of England still using madder dyes.

How I Pack

I've always been rather obsessive about travelling light. I usually try to get as much as possible to fit into a small suitcase, even for longer trips. My packing therefore has to be very efficient, with enough room so that the clothes don't get crushed, and no space is left unused.

For a sartorial traveller, there is the additional difficulty of packing delicate or structured items like suit jackets, hats and ties. This is perhaps where the following 8-step advice will be most useful.

Organize

Without trying to teach anyone how to suck eggs, it's clearly important to lay out everything you're going to pack first, and then separate out delicate or bulky items.

Your bulky items are likely to include a wash bag, several pairs of shoes and perhaps a few electronics, such as a camera. All these items should be packed against the edges of the suitcase, away from each other, with softer things placed in between them.

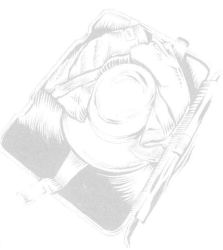

Shoes

Dress shoes need some kind of support inside to stop them being crushed. I use travel shoe trees – plastic forms that are much lighter in weight than the wooden shoe trees you might use at home. They tend to support just the front of the shoe, bracing themselves against the back.

With more casual shoes – or as next-best alternative if you don't have travel trees – small items such as socks can be stuffed inside them to provide a little support.

Each pair of shoes should then be put in its own shoe bag to prevent its surface from being scratched or any dirt coming off into the suitcase.

Hats

Smart hats like a felt fedora or trilby, or a straw panama, are very hard to pack. The slightest pressure on them can change the shape, requiring some work with steam to repair on arrival – or at worst, re-blocking.

Ideally, such hats should be worn or carried in the hand rather than packed. If this isn't possible, or the hat is cheaper and less precious, separate it inside the suitcase, tightly pack soft clothing inside the crown to support it, and then put further cushioning around the outside – knitwear, for example.

This should minimize the amount it can get crushed. As with other points in this guide, it also helps if the suitcase as a whole is fairly closely packed, so there is minimal moving around.

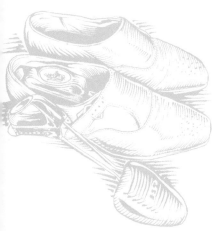

Rolling clothes

Anyone who has backpacked around the world will tell you that rolling clothes is surprisingly efficient when it comes to saving space – and the absence of folds prevents wrinkles.

It's therefore advised to roll casual clothes such as T-shirts, gym wear or sweatshirts, but dress shirts still need to be folded to avoid crushing the collars.

Dress shirts should be folded just as they are in a shop, with the sleeves tucked away underneath and the collar at the top. Folding the shirt around a piece of cardboard will help to prevent the shirt moving around and becoming unfolded, but that's rarely a problem if the suitcase is full.

Folding jackets

Tailored jackets are best packed inside-out to protect the external material from any nicks or scrapes. The following is a good method:

1. Lift up the jacket by the shoulders, with the front facing you
2. Push the left-hand shoulder through its armhole, so it is inside-out
3. Take the right-hand shoulder and place it around the now inverted left-hand shoulder, so the two are cupped inside each other

4. Lift up the jacket with these two shoulders in one hand, and the collar in the other, so that the whole jacket is folded in half along its back
5. Lay it down in the suitcase, and fold it in half the other way

Although this folding method will protect the fabric of a jacket, the biggest issue with packing suits is creases.

Avoiding creases

The best way to avoid creasing is to not use sharp folds. Instead of just folding the jacket onto itself, wrap it around something else, such as a pair of trousers. This makes the fold more rounded.

Often, if I'm packing two jackets into one side of a suitcase, I will turn them inside-out (as described above) and then place them in the bottom of the case, with the bottom halves on top of each other but the top halves sticking out, one on the left and one on the right.

I will then place other soft clothing – trousers, shirts, knitwear – on top, before folding the two jackets around them. This creates a particularly large, rounded fold.

Ties and accessories

Some cases have zip-up sections for small items such as handkerchiefs (folded), business cards or jewellery. It's usually worth putting small things like cufflinks in their own cloth pouch, even inside such a section. Their size makes them so easy to lose.

Other loose items, such as electronic charging cords, are also worth putting in their own bags, for the sake of simplicity and organization.

You can get special cases for carrying ties, but usually these zipped sections in the suitcase are sufficient, if they are long enough. Or simply lay the ties on top of the other clothing, if it is soft. If possible, try to fold a tie only twice, or three times at the most. Rolling ties can work well, but they quickly unroll in the suitcase if the pressure around them isn't even.

Umbrellas are one of the most awkward items to travel with, after a hat. Some umbrella brands make travel versions where the handle and point screw off to enable them to be packed inside a suitcase. Otherwise, bring only a compact, half-length umbrella.

And finally...

Once you and your luggage are onboard, try to get some rest. Even if the plane or train has WiFi, pretend you don't know it exists. Travelling is tiring enough without trying to work or shop online. This is also usually the moment when you realize you've forgotten to pack something important – in which case, you'll have the perfect excuse to go shopping once you arrive!

What I Pack

Although a travel wardrobe is specific to the trip itself – depending on its location and purpose, and the people you plan to meet – the general principles and level of formality outlined here should be appropriate to most journeys.

Travelling

The items on the following pages are what I might pack for a trip of five days: that is, five full days on location, with up to a day of travel either side.

For the travel days, I wear something more obviously comfortable than the tailored pieces I will pack for the other days. I wouldn't sink to jeans and a T-shirt, however – and I also want something to carry my passport and ticket/boarding pass without resorting to my back pocket.

So a sample list of items for summer travel might include:

- Green tailored shorts, from Bardelli
- Navy linen blouson, from Hermès
- Grey long-sleeved Friday Polo from Luca Avitabile
- Tan suede loafers, from Edward Green

For an autumn or winter trip, I might swap Incotex chinos for the shorts, and my favourite navy suede jacket from Stoffa for the linen blouson.

In my hand luggage I will often have a mid-weight piece of knitwear, in case the plane is chilly. I don't like to wear a jacket on the plane, as it can so easily get creased or left behind.

One suit

I rarely travel on a trip of this length without a suit. It's always good to know I have something formal to wear if the need arises – such as an unexpected dinner or event.

This suit will usually be navy or grey, and I will aim to chose one whose elements can also be worn with the two separate jacket/trouser combinations I've packed (see below).

A versatile suit in something like corduroy would be good for travel because the trousers and jacket can be worn on their own with the right partners, or together as a suit. However, such 'three-way' suits tend to be in more casual materials like cotton, and therefore don't fulfil the requirement for a formal look. An exception would be a navy cotton suit, or one made of heavy hopsack.

The suits I therefore usually turn to are my brown Crispaire from Sartoria Dalcuore (whose trousers are quite versatile) or my Anderson & Sheppard grey flannel suit.

Two jacket/trouser combinations

For a five-day trip, I pack two jacket/trouser combinations: two jackets, each with a pair of trousers to be worn with them. If the two trousers can be swapped, or also work with part of the suit (see above), all for the better. As with all pieces for a trip, I try to take the most versatile, functional pieces. Examples would be:

Combination 1:
- Navy hopsack jacket, from Ettore de Cesare
- Tan twill trousers, from Richard James

Combination 2:
- Green-and-black checked jacket, from Solito
- Grey Crispaire trousers, from The Disguisery

The advantage of these four pieces is that each jacket can also be worn with the other trousers. This is not absolutely essential for every piece, however, so one of the jackets could instead be more unusual – for instance, my Liverano purple flannel.

Note also that cream-coloured trousers are probably the most versatile in terms of what they can be paired with. The only problem is that cream trousers are not suitable for colder destinations or for autumn and winter trips. Otherwise, bring them!

With these pieces, plus the single suit above, I have three outfits for the first three days.

On the last two days, I can then wear other combinations of these pieces, or two of the same outfits again (perhaps with different shirts or accessories).

Shirts, ties and handkerchiefs

Shirts in a plain blue are usually the most versatile, followed by plain white – or with subtle patterns that make them no different in effect from plain blue or white.

In order to avoid this being boring, I tend to mix materials (e.g., cotton with linen) or design (e.g., a long-sleeved polo shirt for a tieless day, instead of a button-down shirt). Ideally the shirt collars (whether spread or button-down) are such that they can be worn just as effectively with or without a tie.

My favourite travel ties are navy and black large-knot grenadines. To avoid looking too boring, I would chuck in one or two more interesting options – perhaps a dusty orange Mattabisch.

I always carry two handkerchiefs with me: one in white linen and one in dark silk or wool/silk – e.g., a navy silk from Drake's.

As with the ties, it is also good to bring one bright-coloured handkerchief to add interest – e.g., a yellow-and-cream patterned silk from Rubinacci.

Shoes and socks

There's nothing worse than discovering that one pair of shoes, for whatever mysterious reason, becomes uncomfortable to wear while you're travelling, leaving you with only one other pair to wear every day. Having had that experience, on any trip of more than a couple of days I take a minimum of three pairs of shoes, all brown.

One pair, such as my Edward Green 'Oundles', must be so dark that they can be worn with a smart, dark suit. The others can be mid- or light browns, but, as ever, it's helpful if they can go with multiple pairs of trousers. In the summer, one pair are always the soft, unlined 'Sagan' loafers from Baudoin & Lange; even in the winter, I try to fit in a pair of them as a fourth option.

The socks I pack are pretty much all in my favourite dark green. They go with everything, and they have a little personality – the perfect combination.

Knitwear

I pack at least one piece of knitwear that goes with almost everything. This is usually a mid-weight navy crewneck.

If I have room, I also bring one cardigan in a strong colour such as cream or burnt orange that can add interest to an otherwise versatile (read: dull) outfit.

And last of all: a lightweight scarf. It takes up almost no additional room in a suitcase but makes a big difference on a cold evening.

Illustrations of all these pieces of clothing can be found on PermanentStyle.com

Picture Credits

1 Courtesy Signet
7, 9, 10a, 10b Photo: Jamie Ferguson

Sartorial Travel Tips from the Experts
14 Courtesy The Armoury
16 Courtesy Mats Klingberg
19 Courtesy Anderson & Sheppard
22 Courtesy Wei Koh

Florence
24–25 Photo: Natalia Zakharova © 123RF.com
27, 28r, 32, 34, 35 (all), 36–37 Photo: Jamie Ferguson
28al, ab, 38, 40 (all), 41 (all) Courtesy Simone Abbarchi
29, 42, 44 (all), 45 (all) Courtesy Scuola del Cuoio

Hong Kong
46–47 Photo: iStock.com/Onfokus
49, 51, 54, 57 (all), 58–59 Courtesy The Armoury

London
60–61 Photo: Krisztian Miklosy © 123RF.com
64r, 76, 78–79, 81 (all) Courtesy Anderson & Sheppard
64l, 65, 68, 70 (all), 71 (all), 72, 74, 75 (all) Photo: Jamie Ferguson

Melbourne
82–83 Photo: Robyn Mackenzie © 123RF.com
85, 86, 87, 90, 92, 93 (all) Courtesy Christian Kimber

Milan
94–95 Photo: soloway © 123RF.com
97, 98 (all), 106, 108 (all), 109, 110, 111 Courtesy Stivaleria Savoia
99, 102, 104 (all), 105 Photo: Jamie Ferguson

Naples
112–13 Photo: Enrico Della Pietra/Alamy Stock Photo
115, 124, 126 (all), 127 (all), 128, 130 (all), 131 Photo: Jamie Ferguson

New York
132–33 Photo: Luciano Mortula © 123RF.com
135, 144, 146–47, 149 (all) Courtesy Leffot
137a, 140, 142, 143 (all) Courtesy No Man Walks Alone
137b, 150 (all), 152 (all), 153 Courtesy Paul Stuart

Paris
154–55 Photo: Andrey Kotko © 123RF.com
157, 159, 162, 164 (all), 166, 167, 168, 170 (all), 171 (all) Photo: Jamie Ferguson
172, 174 (all), 175, 176–77 Courtesy Corthay

Stockholm
178–79 Photo: Stefan Holm © 123RF.com
181, 183, 186, 188 (all), 189 Courtesy Skoaktiebolaget
182, 190, 192–93, 194, 195 (all) Courtesy A. W. Bauer

Tokyo
196–97 Photo: iStock.com/yongyuan
199, 201, 204, 206, 207 (all), 208, 210 (all), 211, 212–13, 214, 215 (all) Photo: Jamie Ferguson

Great Shops in Fifteen Other Cities
220 Courtesy Brio
221 (all) Courtesy Optimo
222 (all) Courtesy Linnégatan 2
223 (all) Courtesy Michael Jondral
224 Courtesy Burgos
225 Courtesy Signet
226 Courtesy Kevin Seah
227 Courtesy Wilhelm Jungmann und Neffe

All maps, and illustrations for pp. **229 (all), 230 (all) 231, 233, 235** created by Freddie Denton

Index

Index

About the Author

Simon Crompton's Permanent Style website (**www.permanentstyle.com**) founded in 2007, has become a global authority on luxury menswear. Simon also writes for the *Financial Times*, among other magazines, and is the author of *The Finest Menswear in the World*, published by Thames & Hudson.

To Maria, Lily and Audrey

First published in the United Kingdom in 2019 by Thames & Hudson Ltd, 181A High Holborn, London WC1V 7QX

The Sartorial Travel Guide © 2019 Thames & Hudson Ltd, London

Text © 2019 Simon Crompton

Original design concept by Toby Egelnick: egelnick.com

Designed by Samuel Clark: www.bytheskydesign.com

British Library Cataloguing-in-Publication Data

A catalogue record for this book is available from the British Library

ISBN 978-0-500-02156-9

Printed and bound in China by C & C Offset Printing Co. Ltd

To find out about all our publications, please visit **www.thamesandhudson.com**. There you can subscribe to our e-newsletter, browse or download our current catalogue, and buy any titles that are in print.